Harriet Minter is a journalist, career coach and speaker. She focuses on a variety of issues relating to women, the future of work, media and diversity. She has written for publications including the *Guardian*, *The Times* and *Red*. She founded and edited the 'Women in Leadership' section for the *Guardian*. She has a monthly column in *Psychologies* magazine and hosts TalkRadio's *Badass Women's Hour* radio show and podcast. She is a regular speaker on women's rights, organizational change, workplace diversity and just getting stuff done. She has given two TED talks and appeared on the BBC and Sky News. As well as her media work she coaches individuals to help them achieve their professional goals, and provides big brands with diversity and marketing consultancy.

WFH

WORKING
FROM HOME

HOW TO BUILD A CAREER
YOU LOVE WHEN YOU'RE
NOT IN THE OFFICE

HARRIET MINTER

greenfinch

First published in Great Britain in 2021 by

Greenfinch
An imprint of Quercus Editions Ltd
Carmelite House
50 Victoria Embankment
London EC4Y 0DZ

An Hachette UK company

A CIP catalogue record for this book is available
from the British Library

HB ISBN 978-1-52941-440-0
Paperback ISBN 978-1-52941-441-7
Ebook ISBN 978-1-52941-526-1

10 9 8 7 6 5 4 3 2 1

Typeset by seagulls.net

Printed and bound in Great Britain by Clays Ltd, Elcograf S.p.A.

Papers used by Greenfinch are from well-managed forests
and other responsible sources.

To my home

CONTENTS

CONTENTS

INTRODUCTION

In March 2020, the world shut down. The appearance of Covid-19 forced companies across the globe to close their doors and send their employees home. Businesses were given a choice: let your employees work from home or close. Strangely enough, even those that had spent the previous decade protesting that home working simply wasn't possible in their industry, found a way to adapt. And so those of us who were used to an office-based nine-to-five suddenly found ourselves at our kitchen table, laptop at the ready, desperately hoping our broadband connection could cope with the entire street doing their Monday morning status meeting via Zoom.

Perhaps at the beginning of lockdown it might have been assumed that, as the crisis passed, we would all return to our old working lives, but the longer it went on the less likely it looked. Employees realized that actually not having a commute to an office each day made for a more enjoyable working life. They spent more time with their families and, without the constant water-cooler distractions, they actually managed to get more done. And businesses began to realize that if they could harness the power of home working, not only could they make their staff happier but they could also cut down on the money being spent on expensive offices. There's nothing like the prospect of cutting costs and increasing profits to make a previously untenable idea seem attractive.

So, we all worked it out as we went along. Everyone learned how to use the technology they'd previously avoided, meetings went virtual and the world kept turning. But in the midst of all of this, the bedrock of office life fundamentally shifted and you probably realized you were going to need different skills and to update the way you thought about your career if you wanted both to get ahead and achieve the holy grail of 'work-life balance'. Well in this book, I want to help you do just that.

The longer lockdown went on, the more fans home working started to accumulate. Bosses who had previously doubted their team's commitment realized that productivity was up. Men who had assumed that career success meant sacrificing a family life spent proper time with their kids and decided they liked it. I know one manager who had previously refused to let his team work from home for so much as a morning: two months in lockdown had him swearing they'd never return to the office. Of course, people with caring responsibilities faced more challenges. For those people with children who suddenly found themselves having to balance two full-time jobs, the one they were being paid for and the unpaid teaching role that suddenly came their way, it might have felt as though working from home was an impossibility. And for some of us who thrive off the interaction with others, being isolated and away from our colleagues knocked both our confidence and our enthusiasm. If you found your motivation fell off a cliff during the lockdown period then don't fear, not only are you not alone in this but working from home during a global crisis is NOT the same as working from home in calmer times.

The reality is that given a choice I suspect most of us would want a mix of office time and working remotely. We know that commuting is painful and expensive but sometimes it's worth it to spend time with your colleagues, get away from that pile of ironing and remember that you're part of something bigger than your own living room. Equally, there is nothing like the peace and quiet of a house to yourself when you need to get a project finished, nor the joy of taking a bath at 2pm because you've blazed through your to-do list and nobody will know whether you're still sitting at your desk for the rest of the day or not. And now, with the dubious help of a global pandemic, we have a chance to make that way of life a permanent reality.

The future for work won't be as simple as either being constantly present in the office or always working from home. The options and variations will be endless. Perhaps you'll be remote working – working for an organization but not in the town or country where they are headquartered. You might do flexi-hours, part-time or compressed hours. I suspect that more and more of us will find ourselves working several jobs at once, whether that's as part of the gig economy or with a 'proper' job and a side hustle, or simply two or more part-time jobs blended together.

However you dreamed your working life would look when you were young and hopeful, now is the time when you might actually be able to make it happen. So what are you waiting for? Well, if you're anything like I was back when I was working five days a week in an office, then you're probably worried about the impact that working from home could have on your career. There's that nagging fear that if we work from home we'll either be seen as slacking or it will be a case of 'out of sight, out of mind'. I firmly believe we *can* have it all. We can, and in fact we *need* to design a working life that fits our own preferences and we can climb the career ladder while we do it. And in this book I'm going to show you how.

Planning your career while WFH does pose challenges. For a start there is the simple fact that if you're at home more than you're in the office, it can feel like you're the only one steering your career. You have to go out of your way to find mentors and ask for feedback, because those quick 'catch-up at the coffee machine' moments just don't happen. And if you can't instantly see what your colleagues and peers are up to, or how they're progressing their careers, then it becomes difficult to know how to benchmark your own. In reality, this lack of information can actually be to our advantage. Rather than mapping our career in comparison to others, we have the opportunity to focus on what really excites and drives us, and to figure out how we can get more of that in our working lives. Through this book you'll learn how to plan out your career moves so that not only do you climb the ladder and increase your salary but you also maximize the time you spend doing the stuff you love and are good at.

We'll also look at the practicalities of working from home. You might have made it work while lockdown was happening but balancing a laptop on the arm of your sofa while your flatmates host video calls around you or your toddler demands attention is hardly the ideal long-term working environment. So in this book I'll explain how to carve out space for a home office (even if you're crammed into the smallest room of the house), how to manage your IT/wifi/video call dramas and the simple steps you can take to manage those colleagues who believe out of sight is out of mind. In particular, I'll look at the challenges facing parents – where home is also the office, nursery and sanctuary.

The first step to building a career you love is engaging the help of other people, something that can be hard to do when your nearest colleague is the cat. But remote working doesn't have to mean remote relationships. Whether it's building connections through a Zoom call, using social media to develop your network or finding a mentor without ever meeting them face to face, I want to show you all the ways it's possible to grow your support team without leaving your house. As someone who previously used to get through networking events on a combination of wine and the promise of a takeaway when I got home if I talked to at least five people, moving my networking online has been eye-opening. For a start it requires much less time and judiciously employing the line, 'I don't know about you but I've had my fill of Zoom for the week, shall we do an old-fashioned phone call?' can let you create life-changing connections whilst in your pyjamas.

If you really want to thrive while working from home you need to find your networks and cherish them, not only so you can build your career but also so that you can protect your mental health. This also involves learning how to create boundaries around your work so that you're actually working from home and not accidentally living at work. I know far too many people who thought working at home was the way to bring some balance into their lives and instead found themselves still answering emails while they were getting ready for bed. If we want to create a WFH revolution then we need to avoid these potential pitfalls and I'm going to bring you the best ways to set up a routine, define your limits and communicate all of this with your boss.

And what about if you *are* the boss? Well, this book is here for you too. Managing people is the hardest part of any job but it's made much harder when you can't look those people directly in the eye. So we'll discuss how to hold appraisals, allocate work and give feedback – good or bad – to a team who might be based all around the globe. I've spoken to managers at some of the biggest companies in the world, as well as those with just a few employees, to find the best ways to build a high-performing team no matter where they are. By the end of this book you'll know how to build a team culture without the need for after-work drinks and you'll have addressed some of your own unconscious beliefs around what makes a good employee too.

This book is designed to be a guide for you as you work your way through your career. Some parts of it might be more useful to you now than others but my wish is that you keep coming back to it, using it to adapt and refine your working life until you have created the one that works best for you. As an ambitious extrovert who loves working from home, I want to make sure we can all shape our working lives so that they work best for us, without our choices impacting our career trajectory. As Hillary Clinton said, 'It is past time for women to take their rightful place, side by side with men, in the rooms where the fates of peoples, where their children's and grandchildren's fates, are decided.' Today those rooms are in our own homes, and we deserve to be heard there. So, let's get started.

CHAPTER ONE

WORKING FROM HOME: THE REALITY

So, you've decided to shake up your working life and spend more of it from the comfort of your own home and less of it stuck on a commuter train or in a queue of traffic that literally seems to be going nowhere? Well, congratulations and welcome to the club! Post a global pandemic that saw millions of us having to adapt our working patterns, there's been a rise in those working from home the world over (during the 2020 pandemic, working from home in the UK rose from 6 per cent of the working population to nearly 50 per cent, in the US the number went from 5.2 per cent to 42 per cent, and in Europe it shot up from around 4 per cent to 88 per cent!) and, as a result, a whole new world of challenges and opportunities awaits. This book is here to guide you through some of the issues you will face – but before we get started, there are a few myths and fears that we need to dispel, as well as some key benefits that you might have missed out on while deciding which Ikea desk to purchase.

When we think about making the choice to work from home, most of us will assume the benefits are largely lifestyle-led. We think that it's about the ability to perhaps spend more time with our family, to save ourselves being stuck in the office waiting for our boss to leave on a sunny evening or to avoid spending huge sums of money just on travel. There are some clear lifestyle benefits to working from home, and we'll talk more about those in this chapter, but when we look at it overall, we can see that there are some serious career benefits too, which often get overlooked. In fact, I'm going to show you that working from home can actually progress your career *faster* than a traditional office-based nine-to-five.

First of all we're going to dispel some of the fears you might have about working from home. Too often, people have a traditional view of the request to stay away from the office. Because working from home has often been associated with mothers needing to balance childcare and work, or to those with an ongoing illness needing to prioritize their health, it can sometimes be viewed – incorrectly – as being about some- one choosing to put a pause on their career.

This view stems from an incorrect but pervasive belief that we're at our most productive when we're in the office. At some point in our career, nearly all of us will have thought or been told that if our boss can't see us working then we're not really working, no matter how productive we're being. We've linked presenteeism to productivity and those mental links have proved hard to break. Even now, when we've all faced periods of being forced to work from home, most of us will probably still believe that it's the person who is in the office the longest who will be getting that promotion the fastest.

There's a deep irony in our commitment to the nine-to-five in today's working world. The concept of a 40-hour week based around set hours gained traction over 100 years ago when Henry Ford decided it enabled the highest level of productivity amongst the workers in his car production plants. Fast forward to today and far fewer of us are working on production lines, and yet our working lives still mimic this system. Most of us now are not doing repetitive tasks alongside others, like a cog in a machine. If we want a truly modern way of working, we need to think about whether eight hours a day is really the best way for us to work. And if we are going to do eight hours, do we want to do them between the hours of 9am and 5pm, and from the same place every day?

I know some people who love this system but for most of us – and given that you've picked up this book I'm assuming you too – it's just not a very satisfactory way to live. Working from home allows you the privilege to start to define the daily patterns that suit you best. Perhaps you'll want to do the same hours in the same place every day, or maybe you'll want to mix it up. As you go through this book, you'll learn about your working style and how to flex it. You'll become part of the working revolution. And once you find a work life that works for you, you'll quickly see how your career can blossom.

Let's start by addressing some of the reservations you
might have about working from home.

The 'What if everyone assumes that I'm working from home because I don't care about my career?' fear

This is the number one fear that people mention when I talk
about working from home. Despite huge advances in technology, decades of leadership development trying to convince
CEOs to empower their employees and the working-from-
home test case that was 2020, most of us still believe that if we
put our heads above the parapet and say we want to step back
from the office permanently, our boss is going to assume we're
no longer ambitious.

We think they're just going to hear, 'I am not that focused
on my career. I actually just want to have a better work-life
balance.' The good news is this is starting to change, but if that
change is going to stick we need to be purposeful and strategic. That means being crystal clear with your boss: 'When I
say I want to work from home, this doesn't mean that I'm not
ambitious. It doesn't mean that I am not focused on my career.
What it means is I know the way to maximize my productivity
is by having the flexibility to choose my working space.'

Prior to Covid-19, senior executives were convinced that
allowing their team to work from home was a shortcut to
bankruptcy. Yet after being forced to do it themselves during
lockdown, they suddenly became reluctant to return to the

office when the option was there. Banks that had protested that the technology simply couldn't be safely deployed outside of their buildings suddenly found a way to make it work when faced with the prospect of losing billions of pounds. Lawyers who had been so wedded to the office that anyone wanting to work flexibly was automatically taken off the partnership track, suddenly found senior partners showing no desire to ever come back to their very expensively outfitted workspace. And even those very well-known tech companies that claim to love flexibility but still offer every incentive they can to keep their staff in the office night and day couldn't tempt employees back. Suddenly employees at all stages in their career, including those at the very top, were waking up to the benefits of working remotely.

So, clearly a desire to work from home isn't related to whether or not you're ambitious; it's related to the fact that sometimes being at home with a bit of peace and quiet beats commuting, colleagues and too-cold air-conditioning. We now know that working from home is not a sign of a lack of aspiration but actually just a personal preference. And if you have a boss who doesn't believe that, take yourself off to your boss' boss immediately and take it up with them (see page 51 for a strategic guide to these conversations).

For those of you who want to work from home because of childcare commitments, you have every right to do so. Having a child might make you less ambitious for your career or it might not. It might mean you want to work harder on certain areas and take your foot off the pedal for others. For the majority of parents I've worked with, children have given them a laser-like focus when it comes to figuring out what matters at work and what really doesn't. If anything, the parents I've worked with have been more reliable workers than the rest of us. But if you find your boss making comments about working from home being a sign that parenthood has changed you, then it's time to change them. A workplace that doesn't understand that you can be both a parent and a high-performing employee isn't fit for the future.

The 'I'll never get promoted' fear

Linked to the fear that we'll appear unambitious is the fear that when it comes to promotion, it will be out of sight, out of mind. Being honest, this does happen. If you're going to work from home regularly then you're going to have to make doubly sure that your boss knows what you're up to and is reminded of your brilliance on a regular basis. You need to get good at not waiting for your boss to think of you but actually telling them to promote you (in lots of devious ways). We'll look at how to do this in detail later but right now I want you to honestly answer this question: if you asked your boss now what you wanted for your career in the next five years, would they know?

We are all mostly focused on ourselves yet we forget our bosses are exactly the same. They're just concentrating on their own journeys. If you're not explicitly telling them and telling them *regularly* what you want for your career, they're probably going to make assumptions based on what they know about you. I know a lot of women in their early thirties whose bosses made the assumption that they would be more interested in having kids than promoting their career. Not for unkind reasons; simply because they have seen it before, and they thought that was what was going to happen again.

If you're really good at your job, your boss might assume that what you want is the next promotion. Whereas you might be thinking, 'I want to move into a different department.' Or, 'I want to be doing something different with my work.' Whatever your situation, you need to help your boss help you, so start talking about what *you* want.

The 'What if I accidentally sit down on the sofa, never get up and fail to get any work done ever again?' fear

A very human trait is to divide ourselves into binary groups. We're either people who work hard or we're lazy. Once we've decided which one we are, we then tend to assume that this trait will always appear, regardless of anything we do to counteract it. We become a slave to our own definition of ourselves. This leads to a lot of people who are considering working from home instantly stopping themselves because they fear that they'll never get off their backside unless their boss is keeping an eye on them (or, conversely, that they'll never stop working – see the next section if that's you). Neither of these fears is true and yet despite this I constantly hear, 'If I worked from home, I'd never get anything done. I'd get lost in a Netflix hole and the next thing I'd know I'd be unemployed and wondering where a year had gone.'

Look, that might happen. Maybe. Possibly. If you're really unlucky and possibly dealing with some other issues that you might want to talk to someone about. The reality, though, is that even the laziest of us gets bored of doing nothing eventually, so I'm here to tell you that if for a couple of days you find yourself getting distracted at about 3pm by the thought of an afternoon nap, that is okay. You are absolutely not alone. In fact I might take a little nap right now.

The point is: it doesn't matter. One of the benefits of working from home is that we can allow ourselves the time and space to work to our own energy patterns. We can actually learn to listen to our bodies and make the most of the time when we're feeling productive but also rest when we're tired. If you work from home regularly and you have never taken a 2pm nap, go do it immediately. Our bodies need to rest. If we don't rest, we can't be productive. We've been conditioned to fight this need for rest and adapt our energy patterns to an office culture that starts and finishes at a certain time, but working from home gives you the freedom to actually work *with* your body's natural rhythms rather than against them. Also, if we're being frank, we've all had days where we have sat in the office, stared at our computer screen and achieved absolutely nothing. We need to be honest about that. We need to be honest about the fact that sometimes we've 'rested our eyes' in the loo at work. That's okay too.

One of the reasons that you might find yourself achieving less when you first start working from home is less to do with laziness and more to do with procrastination. 'I'll write that report but first of all I just want to put this load of laundry in/ tidy my wardrobe/fully master the art of baking sourdough.' Procrastination might look a lot like laziness but it's actually a very distinct problem and generally stems from a fear that our best efforts might not be good enough. When we're in an office we have the fear of being seen to be doing nothing to force us into productivity but when it's just us alone with our houseplant, how do we manage it then?

Firstly, when you find yourself procrastinating, rather than berating yourself for it, have some self-compassion. Even the most motivated of us have days when we're just not feeling it. Then have a look at what you're actually procrastinating *about*. Are you putting off getting started on writing that report or are you putting off producing a perfectly polished, deeply researched report? If it's the latter, make a deal with yourself that you'll spend 30 minutes on the report and that the aim of that 30 minutes isn't to get it perfect but just to get something down on the page. If, after the 30 minutes, you want to go back to making the important decision of what colour to paint the bathroom you can, but you have to do 30 minutes of writing first.

I suspect you'll find that once you've given yourself permission to do a slightly less than perfect job, you'll actually find it much easier to get going. And once you're going, you'll find it much easier to get to the end point.

The 'What if I can't stop working and spend my entire life at the mercy of my email?' fear

As much as I'm an advocate for working from home, I can acknowledge that there is something incredibly comforting about leaving the office. That moment when you switch off your computer, put your coat on and officially close the door on the working part of your day. And so it's easy to understand why some people worry that bringing work home might mean that they lose that delineating moment, the moment when they can firmly stop working and start living. This is a legitimate problem.

I've coached lots of people as they switch from full time in the office to a more flexible working style and one of the things they find hardest to adapt to is learning how to switch off. Particularly those with big ambitions for their career – they're already worried that they're not doing enough and so the temptation to keep working long past the time when they should have put their slippers on is hard to resist.

Quite often this ambition is used to justify a level of hardcore perfectionism. If you're someone who can't let go of a project until it's 100 per cent perfect or who looks back at every completed task with a slight sadness that it could still be better, then there's a strong chance you're going to find working from home tough to begin with. The good news is that it's also going to be the most important learning experience for you. Because the only way you can work from home and still maintain a life if you're one of these people is by becoming excellent – 100 per cent perfect, you might say – at setting boundaries. We'll look at how to do this in more detail later in the book but if you already know this is an area of development for you then don't worry, I've got you.

Learning to set clear boundaries around work and the rest of your life is crucial for good mental health. In this book we're going to spend some time investigating where you need to draw these boundaries and how you maintain them. We'll look at techniques such as setting timers on your laptop and blocking access to your email after a certain time. And we'll talk about how you can bring flatmates and family into the quest for better balance. Most importantly, we'll look at why switching off is so hard and what you need to let go of if you're going to make working from home work. The good news is that this fear, unlike most of them, is a place for serious learning and growth. Master this one and you'll be set not just for your working life but for your overall wellbeing too.

The 'What the hell do I do if my kids are at home?' fear

The one caveat to the brilliance of boundaries is kids. Kids are not as keen on respecting boundaries as the rest of us, as parents trying to work from home and look after small people can attest. The reality of working from home as a parent is that as much as possible you want to avoid trying to do double duty as a full-time employee and a full-time parent. Just because you're working from home is no reason to feel guilty about employing all the childcare services at your disposal – you wouldn't feel guilty doing this if you were in the office and this is no different. You wouldn't expect to take your child to a meeting and have them sit quietly in the corner so it's unlikely to work with a Zoom call either.

The main problem with trying to work from home and look after children at the same time is that kids assume that if you're in the vicinity you're available for playtime. One of my favourite genre of YouTube videos is 'professional person being interviewed on the news about their job only to be inter-rupted by their kids'. Strangely enough, most kids are smart enough to know that the absolute best time to get their parent to agree to that one thing they've so far refused is when they sit in front of their carefully orchestrated bookshelf, trying to discuss global economic policy on live TV.

One of the ways you can help kids understand the differ-ence between you being at home and you working from home is by keeping to those clear boundaries you're going to set around what is and what isn't working time. Think about ways you can help them understand this. Can you create a zoned-off space in the house that is your work area, so that you can tell your children that when you're in it you can't be disturbed? Or can you mark your working hours on the calendar so they can see them, or install a countdown clock in the kitchen so they know when you'll be finished?

This clarity works both ways. If you know your kids will get home from school at 3.30pm and be famished and demanding food, then block that time out of your diary so your boss isn't putting meetings in there. There's a reason the subheading for this book is 'how to build a career your love' – it's because you get the chance to design your working life in a way that enables you to function smoothly in both your work *and* your life.

Mostly it's about clear communication, with your kids, your family, your boss and your teammates. When we're clear with people about our boundaries, they will, as much as possible, respect them. So start thinking about what the boundaries are that you're going to want to set and enforce them with yourself now, even if you're still entirely in an office.

The 'What if my team think I'm slacking off?' fear

All my experience suggests that we are capable of working as hard, if not harder, from home than we are in the office. However, other people might not see this as clearly. When we're in an office together we all know who is there first in the morning and last at night, but when we can't physically see this we start to wonder if anyone is doing anything at all. To counteract this, all home workers need to be communication gurus. Building those team relationships, making sure everyone is aware of what you're producing and ensuring collaboration across projects requires first-class comms. It's hard – but getting good at it will be a boost to your career wherever you're based.

During the 2020 coronavirus period I actually spent six months working with a new, and entirely virtual, team. I joined the team six weeks into lockdown, my contract lasted for six months and during that entire time I never once met any of them in person. What this taught me was that the biggest problems arise when we don't know what other people are contributing. And this problem is easily solved: set clear tasks at the beginning of the project, assign each task a co-ordinator and a deadline, and then hold regular check-ins. Sounds simple, right?

In reality it actually is simple, it just requires commitment. Think about how often you communicate with your team and your boss when you're in the office. You probably have a check-in in the morning when you arrive, you'll throw questions across the desk or see them leave to meetings during the day, you'll have 'official' one-to-ones with team members or scheduled project catch-ups, and as you leave you'll probably tell them how much more you have to do or how relieved you are to have finished. All day, each day we're giving our team little prompts to let them know how we're doing and when we're suddenly apart from each other it can be hard to know how to replicate that.

We'll look at how to be a remote manager to a team later in the book but for now here are the basics to ensure you and your team stay connected:

1. The morning check-in: you might want to run this as a video conference but you could also do it via WhatsApp or email. Simply ask your team to let you know what they're working on that day and how they're feeling about

it. Encourage them to ask for and offer help to each other, set it at a specific time each day and ensure you take part too. If you're working across time zones you could do this via Slack or WhatsApp and make it part of the team culture: when you log on for the day you check in with the thread and tell people what you're up to.

2. Use the three connections rule. Each week you want to achieve the following three points of contact:
   i. One 'official' connection – so a status report to your boss or from a team member.
   ii. One casual connection – a quick chat with a co-worker or team member.
   iii. And one random connection – talk to somebody outside of your team, follow up on potential business or reach out to somebody you admire and would like to connect with.

   If you do these three things each week you'll find being out of the office really doesn't mean being out of the loop. Do each three every day and watch your career soar.

3. Use a project management tool to check progress. Whether you buy in specialist tech for this or simply set up a spreadsheet with key dates and deadlines on it, having a system that allows your team to mark their progress against bigger goals, and for you to do the same, means that everyone is on the same page with what work is being done.

It's not just your team that you need to think about when it comes to communication – how you make sure your boss is aware of what you're up to is equally important. I think there's a real advantage here in working from home. When you're in the office it can feel unnatural to wander up to your boss' desk and try to nonchalantly mention how well your recent deal has done or similar. When you're working from home this simply becomes an email with a 'just wanted to keep you up to date…' starter line. Easy. And when it comes to pay-rise discussions you have a ready-made paper trail.

I know, I know, you don't want to send them a bragging email either. But if you don't tell them, they will not know. They cannot see it. You have to be proactive in telling them. Working from home is a really great opportunity for us to actually practise the art of bragging to our boss. You can go from your boss barely knowing your name when you're in the office to their being aware of every brilliant thing you do when you're working from home. It just takes one email.

The 'What if I miss out on what's going on in my industry?' fear

Annie Nightingale has been a DJ on BBC Radio 1 for 50 years. Each morning she wakes up and downloads a playlist of new music. Occasionally she'll listen to something she's heard before but for the most part she wants to know what's new and she goes out looking for it. When she started her career, people would send her records, then tapes, then CDs and now she creates her own playlists. She is 80 years old and still one of the most popular DJs on a radio station aimed at those in their teens. If she can do it, you can do it.

Start following leaders in your industry on social media, set up Google alerts for key terms so you can keep up to date with the news and spend some time thinking about how it might impact your sector. Then share your learnings with everyone on your Slack or WhatsApp channels.

Or if your real fear is that you're going to be cut off from the wider world then make an effort to get out there and engage in it. Working from home doesn't mean you have to stay at home. Go to industry events, find a shared workspace where there are other people to talk to, or even just head for your local coffee shop and make friends with the regulars. Some people might not be cut out for working from home 24/7 and that's fine but being out of the office is no excuse for being out of the loop. Which leads us to...

The 'What if I get lonely?' fear

We need to acknowledge that everyone gets lonely working from home sometimes. There are some who are committed introverts who are always happier in their own company, but I suspect that those people have actually already geared their working lives in a way that suits them. For others, working from home can feel as though they never leave the house. Believe it or not, sometimes the office can feel like a rest, particularly if your home life consists of looking after small children.

For the rest of us, we need human interaction. We need to talk to people. We need to smile at people. We need to feel like we have been seen and heard every single day. You can't get that if you're working from home by yourself permanently, no matter how many Zoom calls you do. But here are some things to remember if you're worried that home working equals loneliness.

Working from home does not have to mean that you are stuck purely in your house. Can you work from a place where there are other people, but perhaps not colleagues? These don't have to be people you have an in-depth chat with but just friendly faces you can say hello to, pass the time with and get to know a little bit. I have become very good friends with the barista in my local coffee shop since I started working from home, as well as about ten other freelancers who all frequent the same coffee shop.

Working from home can still be a social experience. The reality of the world now is that more of us are working from home so if you're sitting there wishing you had someone to chat to your neighbour probably is too. You might want to think about setting up a local meet-up, whereby you find people in your area and you work together for a period of time. If you can't do that in a physical space, you can think about creating Zoom working sessions. I know a group of writers who do a co-writing session via Zoom each morning at 8am. They do a five-minute check-in and then put their heads down and write in silence for an hour. At the end of the session they let each other know how they've got on and offer support, then they go their separate ways. Another friend of mine runs a weekly Google Hangouts for small business owners – they get together for an hour, one person gives a talk about something and then everyone pitches in questions and ideas. They all work remotely but each week they have a space where they can come together with others.

However, if you are continually feeling lonely when working from home then you need to look at what is going on behind that. Natalie Lue, a coach and relationships expert, says that when we feel lonely it's actually because we feel we can't truly express ourselves to anyone. Feeling lonely at work has less to do with how many people are in the office space with us and more to do with whether or not we feel we can open up to them without being judged. Can you be vulnerable with your colleagues? Are you able to tell them when things aren't going well or to ask for help when you need it? If you can't, then you're going to feel lonely inside or outside of the office.

If you are feeling loneliness in your working life, my first suggestion is not to look at how you can surround yourself with lots of people, but to think of the one person to whom you can talk openly. Can you find someone you can open up to about your fears, hopes and worries surrounding work? If it's not someone in your team, do you have a friend or family member who could listen? Or if not, can you find a therapist to talk to? Allowing ourselves to be seen and heard is the number one cure for loneliness. It's not going back into the office.

The 'I can't afford to work from home' fear

One of the reasons that working from home has risen in recent years is because the cost of office space in large cities has also risen. It's become untenable for big businesses to keep all their employees in one office, and they've seen the financial advantage in allowing some of us to work remotely.

Working from home can mean incurring costs, so if your company is actively seeking to encourage its employees to work from home then you should talk to them about how they can cover some of these costs for you. Can they pay for a laptop or home computer? What about a desk or supportive chair? Think about the things you're going to need to successfully work from home (see the list on page 40) and talk it through with your boss.

Also, remember that you might be able to put some of these expenses against tax if you're working from home – check your local regulations. Talk to a good accountant about this but depending on how your company pays you, and your tax bracket, some office equipment could be offset against your tax payments.

Hopefully that's alleviated some of your fears about working from home, so now we get to talk about the good bits! Because working from home is, in my opinion, a shortcut to productivity and balance. Here's how.

Increased productivity

Here are some facts you might be surprised to learn about how we work most efficiently:

1. Productivity peaks at about 40 hours a week. If you're working more hours than that you might be spending more time at your desk but you're getting less done. So all those hours you've spent working late have in reality just been making you less productive the next day, meaning you spend more hours working late and so on and so on.

2. Productivity is not linked to a particular time or place. There is no magic morning routine that will make you more productive if you're a night owl. Nor will working from the peace of a library help you get that project finished if you need to feel the buzz of people around you. We're each unique and work better under different circumstances. The joy of working from home is that you get to set the conditions that work best for you.

3. To maximize your productivity, you need to know what your priorities are and be focused on working towards them. One of the benefits of working from home is that you're less likely to find yourself distracted by other people's priorities. Don't want your colleagues to drag you into another project until this one is finished?

Simply turn on your 'out of office', put your head down and get on with your work. No one is going to appear at your desk to distract you.

When we talk about productivity, what we're mainly talking about is the elimination of distractions and that is much easier to do from home. Think about it: on an average working day you'll turn up to the office, switch on your computer, load up your emails and start trying to catch up on any you missed from the day before. While you're doing that, your colleague will come in and sit down next to you. You'll have a bit of a chat with them. Perhaps you'll go and get a coffee together, leaving a pile of unread emails for later. You'll get back to your desk meaning to carry on with those emails but someone will drag you into a meeting. You'll leave that meeting with a piece of work that you decide to get done immediately, putting off whatever it was you wanted to prioritize this morning. Perhaps you'll have a conversation with somebody who was in the meeting. You'll go for a walk together. You'll discuss what was said. And so it goes on, until the day is finished and you leave the office making a mental note to pick up the unfinished work tomorrow.

I'm not saying that working from home is the cure for distraction – we can all find plenty of things to be distracted by when we're at home, too – but it can really help. Having the space to focus solely on your own priorities and nobody else's means you get to decide how to achieve your day's goals and then you can just do it. You'll find your productivity soars.

Freeing yourself from comparison

This book is about how to build a career you love. We're not talking about how to build the career that your teachers wanted for you, the career your parents wanted for you, the career your best friend has. No. It's how to build a career that *you* love. In order to do that, you need to get clear on your personal goals and ambitions. That can be quite difficult to do in an office where we find ourselves in constant competition with someone else. Perhaps you were hired at the same time as Sarah who sits next to you. You have similar roles. You are progressing at the same rate. Maybe you're actually really good friends. You enjoy working together, but you start to measure your success against Sarah's. Sarah brings in a huge deal; you have to bring in a huge deal. Sarah gets promoted; you have to be promoted. Sarah gets a pay raise. You have to get a pay raise. It can become very easy to spend our career focusing on what someone else is doing rather than carving our own path.

This constant career comparison can be deadly for our career happiness. Rather than pursuing our own dreams, we start to follow other people's career paths. We see someone who moved from a creative role to a strategic one, they're earning more and people are giving them more respect, so we decide we'll do the same – forgetting to check in with ourselves whether it's what we really wanted.

When you spend less time in the office a really interesting thing happens – it's like your brain turns off its comparison tracker. If you want to double down on this effect, I can heartily recommend turning your social media off for a couple of months as well. You stop comparing yourself and actually decide whether or not you're enjoying the task you're working on. You can start to ask yourself what you want more and less of in your daily working life without worrying about what the person next to you would do.

It's very easy in our career to get distracted by what our colleagues and competitors are doing. Working from home takes that distraction away. You're not seeing them every day. You are not being exposed to the latest thing that they're up to. Instead, you have the time and space to really focus on yourself. That means that you can start to map out and achieve your own career goals.

You can start to make moves that actually represent what you want from a job, how you want to work and who you are. From this you can build a career you love. And once you have a career you love you'll find that it starts to expand into a life you love.

A more balanced lifestyle

I always want to make sure that people realize working from home isn't just a lifestyle choice; first and foremost it should be a career choice. That said, there are some big lifestyle advantages that come with it and I don't just mean the ability to spend all day in your pyjamas.

In our 'always on' world, many of us don't have a good work-life balance. We spend too much time working and not nearly enough time living. But if you're ambitious about your career then there is an element of acceptance that sometimes work is going to have to take priority.

Working from home, however, gives you the flexibility to flip between work and life much more easily. Take out two hours of commuting each day and it's much easier to make space for exercise. Live near your kid's school and it's much easier to pick them up when you're working near it too. Rather than spending weeks waiting for a plumber whose working hours coincide with a day you can take off from the office, you can get your washing machine fixed at your own convenience. Some of these things are small but add them all up and they make a big difference to our overall happiness. And we know that happier people tend to also be more productive. Who knew that simply not having to fit your schedule around the plumber's could make you better at work?

As more and more people opt to work from home, many employers are rethinking how they see their employees. Previously bosses assumed that their staff had a life outside of the office but didn't expect them to bring it into the office, but now we're happier to talk about what is going on for us in our actual lives. Employees are becoming humans. And as this continues, so workplaces will flex more. It's much harder for a manager to deny you the right to leave early to pick up a child from school if they know that child's name and have seen them running around in the background of a video call just the day before. Plus, employers are smart enough to realize that if they want to retain the best talent they need to be able to provide a working style that enables that talent to succeed.

Whether you want to work from home because it suits you or you're being forced to do so because your company's office policies are changing, it can have a serious benefit for your career. So now you know *why* it's going to work for you, let's look at *how* it's going to work.

One thing to note: as you work through this book, you will be 'working' through this book. At the end of every chapter will be questions and exercises to think about so it might be worth investing in a notebook specifically for this. Think of it as your career planning diary. As you answer the questions posed here, you'll build up a clear picture of where you want to go in your career and what you need to do to get there. It's useful to have that in one place.

Questions to think about

- What are the benefits to your career of working from home?

- What are your fears around working from home and how will you manage these? (Give a practical example, e.g. if you're worried about being left out of important meetings, can you commit to a weekly one-to-one with your boss so you can ask them if there's anything you need to be a part of that you currently don't know about?)

CHAPTER TWO

WORKING FROM HOME: THE BASICS

Now we've addressed why working from home can actually be a good thing for your career, we need to look at how to make it work for you: in other words, the practicalities of moving your office to your home. In this chapter I'll show you how to convince a reluctant boss, manage the transition with your team and offer some simple tips and tricks for finding the tech that makes virtual communication work for you.

To begin with, though, we need to think about the style of home working you're going to be doing. For most of us, working from home full time won't be an option; instead we'll find a form of flexible working that mixes office hours with working from home, and maybe lets us move our hours around to accommodate our working styles.

Some things to think about when looking at the level of flexibility you want from your working life:

- Are you juggling work and family life?
- Do you work across different time zones? Is your home based in a different time zone to your office?
- Will you have fixed hours or is when you work up to you?
- How often will you be going into the office and how much time will you spend at home?
- What is your home set-up like? Do you have space for a separate office or are you working from your sofa?
- Will you be sharing your home with other people and what does that mean for your working capabilities? For example, will it be easy for you to do conference calls in the kitchen or will there be three other people in there trying to make lunch at the same time?
- If you're going between home and the office, what do you need to do to make sure you have access to all the files/systems and so on that you need in order to be able to do your job?

Thinking about these things before you even start to work from home will ensure that you create a set-up that has the best chance of working for you in the long term. We'll look at some of the issues in this chapter but I'd also suggest chatting to any colleagues or friends who regularly work from home and getting their feedback on what works for them. When we're planning a move out of the office we tend to focus on the big stuff (such as how we will keep in touch with our team or what tech we will need), and forget about the smaller things, such as what we do if our email crashes and how does one politely tell one's flatmate to turn her music down when one is on a Zoom call? Here are some of the practicalities you'll need to address before you can efficiently work from home:

Your colleagues at home

The most important thing you can do before you start working from home is look at who else is going to be in your 'work-space' and how you will manage them. In an ideal world we'd all have enough space in our home environments to have a separate office and we'd live with people respectful enough to know that when we are in our 'office' they must not disturb us, but sadly I've yet to meet a two-year-old who understands that a closed door means Mummy doesn't want their company.

The problem can be exacerbated if you still live with your parents. It doesn't matter how high up the corporate ladder you climb, your mum is always going to assume that you're still a teenager in need of a snack – a huge benefit when you're halfway through creating a presentation and in need of a sugar hit, not so good when you're actually giving the presentation.

Whoever you live with, it's worthwhile taking some time to set up clear agreements for how you share the space when you're working. Here's how to make it work:

1. As much as possible define your own space. If you have to share a kitchen table or desk with others in your household, decide who gets to sit where and stick with it. As anyone who has ever worked in a hot-desking office

knows, there's nothing more annoying than someone sitting in 'your' space.

2. Discuss what you're going to do for video conferences and Zoom meetings. Do you need a room to yourself? If neither you nor your partner/housemate ever wants to have to do a Zoom call from the bathroom, do you need to share your calendars so you can try to avoid both having meetings at the same time? Putting a protocol in place before you find you have a calendar clash is going to save anyone from feeling as though their work is deemed less important.

3. If you're working from the kitchen, agree mealtimes with the other people in your house. It can be highly aggravating if your partner is trying to whip up a smoothie while you have a Skype call with your most important client.

4. Agree a 'we need a timeout' sign. Working from home with parents, significant others or flatmates is not the same as working in an office with colleagues. You can't just get up and leave at the end of the day and if it gets really bad it's much harder to divorce your family than it is to quit a job. Agreeing in advance that there are going to be times of stress and what you'll do when those times appear is going to save you significant angst in the long term. If only it worked with kids too…

5. Working from home with children present is about as
tough as it gets. If you're lucky enough to have a partner
living with you and also working from home, agree in
advance who is going to be responsible for what, and
when. Define the times you are doing childcare from
the outset and make sure these are clearly marked on the
calendar. Anyone booking a work call during the times
when they are supposed to be doing childcare needs to
have a very good reason why (and some sort of apology
gift for the other parent). If you're doing it by yourself,
try to create a routine with your kids as soon as possible.
Easier said than done, I know, but by teaching them that
at certain times of the day or when you're sitting in a
certain place, you're in work mode, you've got a stronger
chance of bringing them onboard with you.

Sharing our working life between office and home is where
I think most of us will end up. If this is you then you might
want to think about the type of work you do from home
versus the office. The obvious split of this is that work requiring other people and collaboration is done in the office, and
the areas where you need time to yourself is done from home.
This split might not always be so clean, particularly if lots of
your team are also remote working, but it does create a good
mindset for the two environments. You go into the office to be
creative and extrovert, and at home you have the space to be
more contemplative and focused. If you know how you like to
work from each location, then you can start to schedule your

working life to maximize this. Don't waste your time having a Zoom call with 20 people if those same 20 people are going to be in a shared office space in two days' time. Instead use your time at home to plan out the structure of the meeting and the key aims that must be achieved within it, then do the actual meeting in person.

Also, if you're going to alternate between home and the office, think about how you communicate that to your colleagues. Mark it in your calendar in advance so people can easily see where you are when they're organizing meetings. If your working hours differ from the standard nine-to-five, consider putting that in your email signature, thereby managing people's expectations of your response time. If you're worried about facing resistance from colleagues about your working-from-home request – and we'll cover that in more detail later in this chapter – always remember: if you manage their expectations, they won't have much to complain about.

A short word on setting up your space

In an ideal world, we'd all have a separate room filled with office furniture from West Elm, adapted to suit our exact height and to minimize our chances of RSI or the inevitable bad back. In the perfect world, we'd all have one of those very fancy sheds at the bottom of the garden, which is an entire office complete with separate living space, kitchenette and a coffee machine that also froths the milk. For most of us the reality is, at best, a desk in our bedroom and a space to store our laptop in the evening so we can pretend it doesn't exist. Some of us might be making do with working from our bed, although if this is you I'd urge you to think about whether this is viable in the long term. For the good of your back, and the sake of your older self, I urge you to consider finding a shared workspace or at the very least a kind coffee shop that doesn't mind you hogging a table and only ordering one latte.

If you do have a little space at home, you can set up an office of sorts quite easily and with minimal investment. From personal experience I can tell you that it is worth spending money on a desk and chair that work for your height. If you can, buy them in person so you can test them out first. Or at least road-test what works for you and then see if you can find a similar specification online. If you're limited on space, find a desk that you can fold down at the end of the day and give what room you do have to a good chair: your body will thank you. If you're very short on space, the combination of a folding chair and desk is perfect if you're using your living room as an office. You can either put your office furniture away in a cupboard or hang it on the wall; this gives you your space back in the evening and signifies the end of a working day, helping you to switch from work mode to domestic mode. And if you really want to support your back, consider a standing desk. Sitting all day isn't good for anyone and this way you don't have to find space for a chair.

In the same way that some people working from home still like to dress as though they are going into an office, creating a 'work zone' can help you get into a professional mindset when you don't have the buzz of an office to help. There is something about the way our brains work which enjoys the delineation of home and work – even if they're in the same space. Do you come home from the office at the end of the day and take off your 'work' clothes? Well, this is the same principle. Putting on an outfit that makes you feel like you're now in work mode can help turn your brain away from wondering what's in the fridge to getting that report done. And having a zone in your house that is dedicated to work helps you create the effect of commuting – moving from one state of being to another – without having to physically move anywhere.

Even if you can't create an entire zone, think about how you can change the space to make it feel like work. For example, if you're working from the kitchen table, can you put a table cloth on it to signify when it's functioning as a dining space, which you take off when you're working? Or can you use a different chair, one that puts you in a more upright position maybe, for work? If you're still working from your bed then stop! Or at the very least get up and make it first. Find ways to use your interior to help your mind know when you're in work mode and when work has finished for the day.

A few things to buy (or raid the office stationery cupboard for)

We have slightly romanticized the idea of remote work. We think all we need is a laptop and a wifi connection and we could do our job from a beach in Bali. The reality is that in your day-to-day you probably also use a variety of other stationery bits and bobs that you're going to be lost without. A good home office has a ready supply of the following:

- **Pens.** Obvious, perhaps, but there is nothing more annoying than finding yourself without one. Invest in a hundred biros from Amazon and never leave a client meeting without a branded pen and you'll probably be sorted for the rest of your working life.
- **Post-its.** You won't believe how much a part of your working life they are until you're trying to do without them.
- **Notebooks.** You think you keep all your notes on your phone/laptop and maybe you do. But trust me, 95 per cent of you actually don't. Get a notebook just in case.
- **Printer.** Despite it being completely environmentally unfriendly, there will always be one person or organization who only deals in hard copy (anything government-related generally falls into this category). Save yourself unnecessary frustration and just buy one from the get-go.

Get your tech sorted

Working from home shouldn't mean you need to become your own IT department but it will mean that you're going to be more reliant on tech for keeping in touch with your team and colleagues.

First things first, get the basics sorted. You're going to need good wifi and a computer to work from. It's worth spending some time getting to understand the wifi available in your area and how to make the most of it. If you're sitting in the part of the country with the fastest, most up-to-date wifi, then great. But for everyone else, make sure you have enough download capacity to handle any large files that might be required for your work and consider investing in a booster to enhance your signal connection. Also, don't set up your home office in a corner of the house with the worst signal – just a tip from someone who's been there and done that.

When you're thinking about what computer you need it can be easy to go for the flashiest on the market. Curb those instincts though and ask yourself: 'What would work be buying me?' That is the one to get. You want to know that it will be compatible with your work systems, and that your IT team will entirely understand how it works so that when something inevitably goes wrong they're actually able to help you, rather than having to thumb through the user manual of an operating system they don't understand.

If your work requires particular systems or programmes, make sure it's possible to install these on any computer that you'll be using from home. It's worth talking to your company about whether they have a work laptop they can just give you, to save all the agonizing. Most large organizations who are encouraging employees to work from home will have a bank of these sitting somewhere so make friends with the IT team and find out how to get your hands on one.

Side note – making friends with your company IT team is possibly the most helpful thing you can do when you're working from home. You're going to run into all the usual IT problems and without a colleague sitting next to you who had the exact same issues last month and therefore knows how to solve them, you're going to save a lot of time and frustration if you're on first-name terms with Tim on the IT desk. If you're freelance, you won't have a standby IT department, so it's essential you find yourself a decent local tech guru you can call if you're having a computer nightmare – you'll have to pay for the service but you should be able to claim it against tax.

Finally, do you get a home computer, complete with screen, keyboard and the bit that houses all the actual tech or do you get a laptop? There are pros and cons to each and the ultimate decision will probably come down to personal preference but here are some things to think about.

You can configure a home computer to suit you exactly, saving you from the eternally hunched shoulders that come with regular laptop use, and you'll have a larger screen which makes viewing everything easier. However, this very much relies on you having the space for it. If it's going to take over your living room and you'll spend every evening feeling its lurking presence reminding you that you could be working rather than relaxing, get a laptop. If you've got the space to put it in a different room and create a home study, then a home computer could be for you.

The one big advantage of having a laptop is that you're mobile, so working from home doesn't always mean working from home. It could mean working from a coffee shop, the bar, your friend's house, that poor restaurant trying to operate a fast turnover but stuck with five home workers hogging tables etc. If you've got space and money, get a home computer for home and a laptop to give you some freedom. But since few of us have either enough space or enough money, think about how you work best. Do you like structure and routine? Does it suit you to sit down at a desk in the same place each day? If so, you're probably better off starting with a home computer. If you like your freedom and find yourself easily bored if you're in the same place too often, get a laptop.

VIRTUAL MEETINGS

2020 was the year Zoom and video conferencing finally came into its own and if you haven't yet got comfortable with it, then now is the time to do so. While choosing to organize your schedule so that you can be physically present for meetings is the ideal, it's not always going to be possible. We'll look at some techniques later on in the book for presenting yourself in the best way possible on camera but your first priority is getting comfortable with the technology itself. Whether you are using Zoom, Microsoft Teams, Cisco Webex or any other form of video conferencing, there are some key tricks that make it easier.

Minimize yourself. It doesn't matter how enlightened a human being you are, when we see our face on a screen all of us will spend more time looking at ourselves than at the person we're talking to. The easiest way around this is to find the setting that either gets rid of your view of yourself completely or at the very least minimizes your picture. If even a small view of yourself is too distracting, stick a Post-it over the top (aren't you glad you bought some?). If you feel truly self-conscious on camera some video conferencing will let you set a filter. Of course the problem with this is that as soon as someone sees you in person their first thought will be how tired you look. Much better to find a way to not see yourself onscreen and forget what you look like. And if all else fails, remember that the person on the other side of the video call is far too busy looking at themselves to notice you.

Take a break from your screen. If you have ever had to do a workplace health and safety check you'll know that taking a break from your screen is recommended at least every 30 minutes. This is particularly important if you find yourself doing a lot of video calls. Lots of people find virtual meetings more tiring than actual meetings and there is a simple reason for this: they require more concentration. Think about your behaviour at an in-person meeting. You'll probably take some notes, you'll look at the speaker, you might gaze out of the window, note down the ingredients you need to pick up your way home for tonight's dinner and then focus back in when someone says your name. In reality none of us are concentrating for the entire meeting. The problem with video calls is that it's very easy to see when someone's concentration has wandered so we all stare at the screen as hard as we can to prove we're paying attention. Staring straight into the face of someone you're talking to for the entire time you're with them is unnatural behaviour and yet it's the behaviour we try to recreate on a video call. So first of all, give yourself – and your eyes – a break. Take a notebook to any calls and make sure the person on the other side knows you'll be taking notes throughout so they're not offended if you look away. Then, as much as possible, leave ten minutes between calls so that you can step away from your computer and give your eyes a break. One way to do this is to create a 50-minute meeting culture in your office. Set all meetings for this time, rather than the standard hour, and you'll not only get a break in between but you'll start to make them more efficient too.

Go back to the phone call. Never be afraid to say, 'Shall we do this with cameras off?' If you've done too many virtual meetings that day it's quite likely the person you're talking to has as well. Become their favourite person by admitting that you're tired of the sight of your own face and wouldn't it be easier if you just did this meeting as a phone call. I have yet to encounter anyone who is not delighted when I suggest this.

Accept that it won't always be perfect. If you have children at home then you need to concede that your colleagues are going to learn that early on. While you might be able to bribe teenagers to stay in their rooms, toddlers are smart enough to know that mid-meeting is the moment they will get the most attention. There is nothing more you can do here than be upfront with colleagues and clients about what is going on. If your child has decided that now is the moment to pull everything out of the fridge, just as you try to Skype the office from your kitchen, then you're going to have to go with it. If home working has taught us anything it's that nobody's life is perfect, so give up trying to pretend that yours is.

OTHER VIRTUAL METHODS OF COMMUNICATION

From WhatsApp to Slack via G-chat and with a side order of social media, it should be easier than ever to foster communication in the workplace. And yet, our biggest fear when we start working from home is that we might be out of the loop. When you're thinking about how you're going to stay in touch with your team and colleagues, think about breaking down those communication lines into formal and informal channels.

Formal channels are things like meetings or emails. They have a structure to them and are designed around specific workstreams or key performance indicators (KPIs). In a virtual world you can recreate some of these official channels without the need for full-on in-person meetings. For example, you might use project management software such as Monday or Basecamp, or technology like Slack or WhatsApp, to set up specific areas where your team can talk about a particular project or client.

Designing formal communication channels is generally the easy bit; it's much harder to create the informal communication channels that spring up naturally in an office. For example, when you're working in the same place as your team you'll probably check in with them in the morning, ask after their evening or find out what they're up to that day. You might chat while queuing for lunch in the canteen, and you'll analyse a meeting as you walk back to your desk. There are lots of little moments during the day to foster communication and find out what is going on beneath the surface of a company. When you're working from home you can't rely on these happening organically, but you can use tech to help foster them.

The reality of creating informal communication channels is that you have to formalize them. The San Francisco-based software company GitLab has 15 processes for creating informal communication channels but two that I really like are coffee chats and welcoming interruptions. A coffee chat is time set aside each week for a video call of 25 minutes that doesn't have any specific agenda. Much in the same way that you would grab a coffee or lunch with a colleague and have a chat about your lives, this is a way of doing that without having to actually be together. As well as doing it yourself, encourage this within your team. We might think that a meeting without an agenda is a waste of time but it's the simplest way to encourage your team to relate to each other (and you) on a personal level.

Welcoming interruptions is another way of doing this. At GitLab, meetings stop when someone's child or pet wanders into view of the video call. They deliberately make time for the personal elements of life, which are seen when a colleague works from home. They're curious about what is on their bookshelf and want to know the names of their colleagues' children. As with coffee chats, it's a way of encouraging a level of intimacy between colleagues, even if they're not in the same physical space.

Emma Sexton, the founder of UK-based creative agency MYWW, has an entirely remote team. To foster a feeling of community they have Slack channels set up for general chit-chat – what they watched on TV last night or what's going on in the news, for example. They also have a daily 'How are you?' check-in, where team members actually talk about what's going on with themselves as well as what's going on with their specific projects. The key is to be explicit about wanting to invest time and effort in building those relationships with your colleagues rather than hoping it will manifest of its own accord.

One way you can use tech to help you here is to use video-conferencing technology as though it was an informal chat in the corridor. Rather than a long email chain or setting up a specific meeting, get into the habit of saying, 'Shall we jump on a quick call and talk about this?' and then pinging over a Zoom, Hangouts or Teams link. Not every video call has to be an hour-long, planned-in-advance meeting; a quick check-in is sometimes more effective.

So now you've got an idea of what you need to efficiently work from home, it's time to clear it with your workplace and get ready to leave the office. First of all, you need to talk to your boss about it.

How to tell your boss you
want to work from home

When everyone was forced to work from home, it quickly became apparent that there were two types of bosses in the working world. The first took to working from home with ease. They figured out the best ways to keep in touch with their team, trusted them to get on with their work and created an atmosphere of collaboration and commitment without the need for a physical building. The second type became convinced that nobody was doing any work, attempted to micro-manage and was delighted to get back into the office the second it was opened again. They communicated this delight be sending everyone pictures of themselves walking into the office, making coffee in the office kitchen and taking a selfie from their desk. They also made it abundantly clear that they expected everyone in their team to follow suit.

If your boss falls into the first category then congratulations: having a conversation with them about working from home should be a straightforward affair. They should already be clued up on the best technology to enable home working, know how to monitor productivity and understand that some people just work better outside the office. Remind them of these facts and you'll be good to go.

If, however, your boss falls into the second category then you're going to need a more strategic approach to the conversation. Here's how that strategy goes:

MAKE IT ABOUT THE BUSINESS

The first thing to remember when asking your boss for anything – home working, a pay rise, promotion – is that they care more about the business than they do about you. If you go into this conversation with a long list of reasons why working from home is going to improve your life then your request is almost certainly going to be rejected. Instead you need to think about why it's good for the company as a whole. How will you working from home benefit the business?

If you're not sure, ask yourself the following: will my working from home boost the finances of the company? And if so, how? Perhaps you working from home means that you'll be able to get more done. If so, think about how you can show this – can you give them a direct figure and explain why working from home helps you meet that, for example? Perhaps if you work in sales it's easier to make more calls from home. Or if you're a designer the peace of working from home means you're able to pull together images more quickly. Show how working from home will increase the bottom line.

There are other reasons, too, why working from home is good for business. For example, if your company is going through a culture change and wants to transition to a more flexible environment, you can be a guinea pig for how this works. Offer to work from home as a test case and give regular feedback on how it can work for the whole business.

Or maybe your company is looking at its reputation in the marketplace? Can you compare how your business works with its competitors and make a case for it being seen as more forward thinking if it takes a proactive approach to flexible working? Could it attract key talent if it had a reputation for allowing working from home?

If you're not sure what the priorities are for your business at the moment, see if you can find any recent presentations given by the leadership team around company strategy or five-year plans. Have a read through and assess the key aims and objectives of the business right now, and see how working from home can meet this. As a starting point, if your company is looking to grow then you should focus on productivity and attracting talent. If it's about riding out difficult times suggest how having fewer people in the office could save money or how a reputation as forward thinking could help it attract clients. Whatever you do, make it about the business rather than you.

If your boss tries to suggest that this is your personal life taking precedence over work – if they suggest that you wouldn't be asking for this if you didn't have kids, for example – gently steer them back to why it's good for the business. But also make a note of exactly what they said and the date and time: you're working for a dinosaur who is probably going to try to screw you over in the future. Keep a note now and have an unofficial chat with HR soon.

GET YOUR TIMING RIGHT

While working from home might seem a completely logical move to you, your boss hasn't been giving this the headspace you have, so pick your time to discuss it. Don't fling this on them as they're about to go into a big meeting or at 4pm on a Friday when they're desperate to get home. Find out a time that's going to work for them when they're feeling calm, sorted, they don't have too much on their plate, and they can think about you and your career. Give them a heads-up that this is what you want to talk about when you organize the meeting. If you already know what sort of structure you'd like you might want to mention this but don't bombard them with details beforehand. In summary: approach them when it's convenient for them, tell them you'd like to talk about the possibility of finding some flexibility in your working patterns and then follow up your meeting with a recap of what you'd like as well as the next steps.

DEAL WITH ANY RESISTANCE

Sadly, not every boss is going to be instantly won over by your beautifully crafted argument and if they're not a fan of working from home you're probably going to meet some resistance. First of all, know that if this happens, it's less about you and more about your boss. It's not that they want to make your working life a misery but they're probably worried about how it's going to impact them. It's your job to allay those fears.

In the majority of cases, if your boss is anti-WFH it's because they assume the second an employee leaves their sight they're sitting on the sofa, watching Netflix and achieving nothing. And making their boss look bad in the process. So you need to reassure your boss that even if they can't see you, you will still be productive and you will still be checking in with them. Have a plan for how you're going to do this at the ready; you might want to suggest weekly catch-ups in person or on video calls, a daily email check-in or a monthly written report. If your company uses project management software explain how you'll use this to monitor your own projects and maximize your efficiency. The more you can show them that they'll still know what's going on, the more confident they are going to feel in letting you work from home.

Sometimes a boss just doesn't like working from home out of principle. In these cases it's usually because they tried it themselves, didn't like it and now don't want anyone else doing it. You might simply have to call this out; point out that we all have different working styles and suggest that you'd like to find out what works best for you. You could also suggest that you 'trial' working from home for a set period, with a discussion in a couple of months about how it's working from both sides.

When you're faced with resistance, the key question to ask here is, 'How can I make this work for you/the company?' It's going back to making it clear you're doing the best thing for the business (and your boss) rather than yourself. Also by asking this you're helping to flush out what they're really worried about, which means you can then find the answer that is going to work for them.

Don't expect this to be a one-off conversation. It might be a conversation that takes two or three rounds for you to find agreement. Offer to do a test period and set some clear KPIs with your boss against which you can both measure its success. And if they're still a no, suggest that you review this decision in six months. The reality might just be that it doesn't work for the company or your boss, and then you have to make a choice about whether or not you want to stay with the company. Working from home has to work for both employer and employee but if your company really can't find a way to countenance it and it's become important to you, then it's time to move on.

Telling your team

So, you've asked your boss, now you need to tell your team. While it might not seem as though your team's view on this is as important as that of your boss, your working from home is going to have an impact on them and you should think upfront about how you manage that. If you're the manager of a team then you should be thinking about any concerns they may have and how you'll stay in contact with them when you're not physically present.

Generally when a team member announces they're working from home, the major concerns their colleagues have are: 'Am I going to have to pick up their work? And how do I get hold of this person when I need them?'

Before you actually begin working from home it's a good idea to sit down with team members individually and update them on your plans. Ask them if there's anything they're worried about within this or if they can see any problems arising from it. Depending on their view on working from home, they might be happy for you, jealous or think it's a terrible idea. Just remember that their fears are based on their own beliefs; they're not facts and you don't have to listen to them if you don't want to. But taking them into account and thinking of ways to manage them now is going to save you a lot of hassle later on down the road.

Working from home can be infectious; once you start doing it you'll probably notice some of your team wanting to do the same. This means two things. Firstly, you're now setting an example for how remote working works (or doesn't) and – not to put too much pressure on you – if you screw it up it's likely your team will too. We'll look at how to manage a team remotely in detail later on in the book but for now think about this: if you knew you were setting the standard for everyone working from home, what would you want that standard to be?

Secondly, if you're managing a team that now wants to work from home, make sure you don't pull the ladder up behind you. It might not be possible for all of them to do it but if you're feeling some of the fear your boss felt when you first asked, think about the response you would have wanted from them and go there. Don't become the difficult boss you've just had to overcome.

And you're off...

So that's it. You've cleared it with your boss, got your home office set up just right and are now on your way to a life of remote working. Just remember that working from home is a privilege and right now it's not a privilege that is open to everyone. There can be downsides to it: we might get lonely or miss our colleagues or worry that we're being left out of the business' plans, but the fact that you get to worry about these things at all already marks you out as someone working for a well-meaning organization and blessed with enough goodwill to be trusted outside of the office. There are some jobs where it's simply not possible and some employers that just won't countenance it. You're one of the lucky ones. Now it's up to you to make it work.

Questions to think about

- Who do you share your home space with and what are the discussions you need to have with them before you start working from home? Give yourself a deadline for sitting down with them and talking through your plan.
- What does your boss need to know to be convinced that you should work from home? (Remember: start with why it's good for the company, not why it's good for you.) If you think it's possible you will encounter resistance, prepare your points and rehearse them.

CHAPTER THREE

BUILDING A CAREER PLAN FROM HOME

Much as I wish I could tell you that building a successful career from home was entirely dependent on making sure you had a good office chair and strong wifi connection, it's sadly not that simple. The last couple of chapters have shown you how to get your home office set up and you've found a working rhythm that works for you, so now it's time to think about where you actually want your career to go.

Previously, there has been a tendency to think of working from home as the thing you do when you've 'settled' your career. Perhaps you've reached a point that feels comfortable and now it's more about lifestyle than progress. If that's you and you're happy with that then great, although be aware that just because you think you've found the job that will last you a lifetime it doesn't mean your employer thinks the same – it's wise to still keep building your network and thinking strategically about what your next steps would be if your current job comes to an end. For most of us, working from home is a mix of convenience, choice and necessity – but the point is, it really shouldn't become a career dead end.

So in this chapter, I'm going to show you how you can start to plan out where you want to be in the next year, five or even ten years. Over the course of this chapter you'll build a career plan that has enough focus to keep you on track but also has the flexibility to move with your life – after all, very few of us can be completely certain about what will happen to us in the next ten years. However, if you create a plan, at least you'll be clear on what does and doesn't feel like progress to you, and you'll have a framework of reference for your future moves.

I don't always like rules but they're helpful when career planning so here are some ground guidelines to keep in mind as you go:

1. No idea is a bad idea. So, your dream job is to be the person who finds a cure for cancer but you dropped science at GCSE and have no idea where to start? If it's an idea that lights you up, don't dismiss it out of hand. If there's something churning away inside of you that you keep coming back to then pay attention to it. Perhaps you won't be the research scientist who finds the cure but maybe you'll be the person who raises the money that funds the research scientist. Dreams are good, so hang onto them.

2. This is about building a career you love – so put that
love front and centre. There is an old saying: 'Do what
you love and the money will follow.' I'm not sure I
entirely agree with it as my love of expensive hotels has
only ever taken money from me and never returned it
but sometimes we can let our fear of not having enough
money get in the way of a dream. Get realistic – write
down what you absolutely need to bring in in order
to meet your bills and keep a roof over your head, and
then work out how you can do this and still work in a
career you love. Until you are in a job or an industry,
it's hard to know what the maximum salary available is
so see if you can talk to people in that industry about
earning potential. Don't write off something which
excites you just because you think you can't make it
work financially. There is generally more money out
there than you'd believe, so get your financial ducks in a
row and go test the waters.

3. Don't worry if you don't have the exact job title and
company picked out by the end of this process. As we
go through you'll see that career planning is less about
knowing exactly what you want to do and more about
getting really clear on the feeling of what 'happy in your
career' feels like, so you don't settle for anything less.

Why do you need a career plan?

The average age of retirement in the UK is just under 65 and in the US it's 62, and it's only going up. Most of us started work in our late teens. That means that we spend nearly 50 years, over half of our lives, at work. There is a fairytale sold to us at an early age that if we follow the rules, work hard and behave ourselves, then we too will live happily ever after. In reality, it's not that simple. If you want to be happy in your job then you need to firstly know what makes you happy outside of your working life and then proactively seek out those opportunities in your working life. If you wait for the dream job to come to you, you're going to be disappointed. This is the moment to decide what you want and go after it yourself.

Imagine if you moved into a flatshare and a month or so after moving in discovered that one of your flatmates liked playing loud music at 4am each morning, while you much preferred to spend that time asleep. You wouldn't stay in that situation, would you? Either you'd ask the music-paying flatmate to keep more social hours or you'd move out. And yet hundreds of thousands of us will stay in a working situation we hate simply because we can't believe there is anything different out there.

If you're doing the standard nine-to-five, five days a week, half of your waking hours are going to your job (and let's face it, many of us end up putting in more hours than that). If that job is making you miserable then it's time to rethink how you're spending your time. In this career planning section, the goal is to focus on the things that bring you joy, on the skills you want to build, the experiences you want to have and the values that you want to live by both at work and at home. And if that feels like a lot of work, just remember – staying in a job where you're miserable is one of the most stressful things you can do. Taking a bit of time to decide what would make work good for you will ease that stress, give you a clear focus and put you back in charge of your career and its future. This is particularly crucial for working parents – do you want to be coming home to your family exhausted and demoralized? If your work is making you miserable then you're almost certainly bringing some of that energy home to your family. Taking a bit of time to create a career you love won't take away from them, instead it will energize you and ensure that the time you spend with them isn't filled with work worries.

Building your career

When I talk about career planning, I like to use the phrase 'building a career plan' because that is what you have to do. It's a step-by-step process.

Over the next few pages are a selection of ideas and exercises to help you start to identify what your ideal working life looks like.

First up, we look at **values**. Don't worry yet if you're not sure what your values are or even if you have any when it comes to work (though you definitely do). In this section it's about getting clear on what you love and what inspires you.

So often we take on roles or jobs because someone has told us it's a good option or that to get ahead you have to do a certain thing or behave a certain way. When we examine our values, we make it really easy to be able to identify the things we want in our life and, more importantly, the things we don't want. If you're someone who finds it hard to say no to things, doing some work on your values is essential – when you realize how often you're saying yes to something you don't agree with, it becomes much easier to say no.

Then we're going to look at **skills**, both those you have and those you'd like to acquire or perfect. Often when I ask people about their skills they can tend towards humility but to be honest, humility isn't helpful here. This is the place to big yourself up, shout about your brilliance and be open about what you want. So when you're thinking about the sort of skills you have in your arsenal, be ready to brag. You don't have to show this work to anyone so it's okay to really go for it. Think Mariah Carey levels of confidence.

Once you've got your values and skills sorted, then we'll start to build a **vision**. This is the bit where you can let your imagination run wild. A good idea starts with a vision, a dream. Now you might be the rare person whose entire dream consists of a big chair in an even bigger boardroom but for most of us, dreams are multidimensional, so we're going to look at viewing our career plan through a holistic lens. What that means is that if it's really important to you in your future to climb Mount Everest, then you must put that in your career plan – the two really are linked.

Also remember that this is about creating a vision for the life you want, not an unmovable goal. So if you think that, in five years' time, you want to have a specific job title at a specific company, that's great, but leave some space in there for ambiguity too. Things change, opportunities arise that you could never have predicted; be open to all of that. This is the reason we look at values rather than job titles in this book. So let's start there.

Finding your values

There's a lot in our lives that can change: as we get older, we develop different interests, move areas, have children etc., but at the core of our being are a set of beliefs that govern how we decide to make those changes. These are your values. A colleague of mine says that values are anything which has value to you, but which you can't put in a wheelbarrow. You might value your children but you could also pick them up and put them in a wheelbarrow if they were annoying you. So your own children aren't a value, they're living and breathing beings. But family – the concept of creating a shared community, bringing children into it, spending Sundays sitting around the table together sharing, turning up for each other even when you really don't feel like doing it – that's a feeling, a belief. You know absolutely what it means to you but you can't put it in a wheelbarrow, so it's a value. Does that make sense?

The reason our values are important in our working life is because when we ignore them and take on work which goes against them, we make ourselves unhappy. We've already talked about how half of your waking life is going to be spent working – do you want to be miserable in that half? Probably not, so it's important to find a working culture that fits with your values.

Let me give you an example. If you are somebody who really values freedom, you probably want to be working in a career where you have a lot of autonomy, where you get to make a lot of your own decisions, where perhaps you don't have fixed hours, or you get to move between projects easily. If, on the other hand, you are somebody who really values knowing where you stand, you probably want to work in a more structured environment, where there is clear hierarchy and process.

Both of those working situations are equally valid and needed in this world, but if the person who valued freedom ended up in a process-driven organization, they'd probably find themselves feeling desperately unhappy, even if the job title suggested it should be their dream job. And vice versa.

So let's start by identifying some of your key values. A quick tip before you start: go for the values that your best self has, the self that you really admire. It's easy to think, 'Oh I'd love to have that value but I'm not good enough/not there yet.' Put those thoughts to the side and just go for the ones your best self wants.

First up I want you to write down as many values that you hold as you can think of. Aim for 50 but note down at least 25. I know, that seems like a lot and right now you're having a blank. To help you out, here is a list that you can pick from. This is by no means a definitive list, so do add your own. See the list as a jumping-off point.

Acceptance	Creativity	Greatness
Accuracy	Curiosity	Growth
Achievement	Decisiveness	Happiness
Adaptability	Dedication	Hard work
Altruism	Determination	Harmony
Ambition	Discipline	Health
Assertiveness	Discovery	Honesty
Balance	Drive	Humility
Beauty	Effectiveness	Humour
Bravery	Efficiency	Imagination
Brilliance	Empathy	Improvement
Capability	Enthusiasm	Independence
Certainty	Equality	Individuality
Challenge	Ethical	Innovation
Charity	Excellence	Inspiration
Choice	Experience	Integrity
Clarity	Fairness	Intelligence
Collaboration	Fame	Joy
Comfort	Family	Justice
Commitment	Fearlessness	Kindness
Common sense	Feelings	Knowledge
Communication	Freedom	Leadership
Community	Friendship	Learning
Compassion	Fun	Logic
Competence	Generosity	Love
Confidence	Genius	Loyalty
Connection	Giving	Mastery
Control	Gratitude	Meaning

Motivation	Results-oriented	Support
Openness	Rigour	Surprise
Optimism	Risk	Sustainability
Order	Satisfaction	Talent
Organization	Security	Teamwork
Originality	Selflessness	Thoroughness
Passion	Self-reliance	Thoughtful
Patience	Sensitivity	Timeliness
Persistence	Service	Traditional
Playfulness	Sharing	Transparency
Power	Significance	Trust
Process	Simplicity	Truth
Productivity	Skillfulness	Uniqueness
Professionalism	Smartness	Victory
Purpose	Spirituality	Vision
Quality	Stability	Wealth
Reason	Status	Welcoming
Recognition	Strength	Wisdom
Respect	Structure	Wonder
Responsibility	Success	

Once you've written your list, have a look at the values you've chosen. How many of them show up in your current working life and how strongly do they feature? Are there any that you completely fail to experience in your working life? It's interesting to see which of our values are easy for us to follow and which we are more likely to forget about when we walk through the office doors.

Now, looking at the list of values you have written down, I'd like you pick five that you want to focus on for at least the next year. Think about waking up every day and living your life by those values – which five would you pick? Now write those five out and next to them write three or four values that you feel are within them. We're trying to get to your definition of each word. Let me give you an example.

I had 'freedom' as a very high value. For me the value of freedom could be defined by the words: choice, security, self-reliance and wealth. Remember, that is my personal definition of freedom: if you also chose that as a value it's okay if your definition is very different.

For each of those five words you've chosen you want to create your own definition – this is so that when you make a choice about your career, you can be certain that it is the right one and not influenced by anyone else's opinion either on what you should be doing with your life or what your values mean. Here's some space to write this down:

Value   Definitions

1. _____   _____

2. _____   _____

3. _____   _____

4. _____   _____

5. _____   _____

Have a look at the words you've now written down. How does it feel looking at them? How would it feel to live your life by those words? Good? A bit exciting? Perhaps a bit scary? Any emotion other than bored or uninterested is good here! Don't worry if you feel a bit anxious or scared right now; perhaps you're looking at those words and thinking it's a big shift from your current life? Or maybe you're looking at them and thinking achieving any of them would be impossible? The good news is you're only at the start of the book so you don't have to have any of the answers yet! For now, keep the list of values somewhere you can find it easily. We're going to need them as we build our career plans, so let's go onto the next step.

You have more skills than you think

Now you've got clarity on the values that are important to you, we're going to get a little bit more practical. Remember how I said there was no point in being humble when writing a career plan? This is the place to brag about everything you've ever done and to open your mind to everything you want to do. If you need to gee yourself up for this, now is the moment. Put on some loud music and dance around the room, give yourself a virtual high-five and remind yourself of the things you're brilliant at. Whatever you need to do to get yourself into bragging/sky's-the-limit mode, now is the moment. Off you go and do it; don't worry, nobody is looking and I'll be here when you're ready.

Okay, so now that you're fully geed up, let's look at what skills you have and how you can put them to use.

Skills can usually be divided into three categories: those we have, those we'd like to have and those we have accepted are never going to be our area of expertise. Let's start with those we have.

Looking back over your career, I want you to write down the three things you are most proud of. They don't have to have been big moments, although they might have been, but anything that when you think about it gives you a little glow of pride is acceptable here. I like to write these down, partly because it's useful for the rest of the exercise but also so I can look back on them when I'm having a down day and remember that at one point I did something good. So write each of these moments out. Add as much detail as you can:

1. _____

2. _____

3. _____

Have a read through of each of these moments and ask yourself what skills you were showing in each of them. Perhaps you organized an event that was a big success. What did you need to do to make that a success? There was planning, probably collaboration, you definitely had to talk to people about the event to get them there so that's communication. Perhaps you used social media to promote it. Did you run the budget for it? And you don't have to have been in charge of a project to have used skills on it. Did you have to bring senior management onboard with an idea? That's influencing. Did you have to make sure all of your senior manager's ideas actually came to fruition? That's showing a level of time-keeping and organization as well as attention to detail.

You also have skills specific to your work as well. Perhaps you had to use particular computer programmes or project management tools. Whatever it was, stick 'em down.

If you're completely stuck there is a list below and overleaf to help spark inspiration – it contains mainly softer skills and you will certainly have others which are specific to your industry and role. *Please don't read this list and just circle the skills you use every day.* We're specifically looking for skills that you used on projects that you're proud of. So often we focus on developing a skill because someone tells us we're good at it, rather than because it brings us any joy or excitement. However, if we look for the skills we used on projects we're proud of, those are often the ones we enjoy the most or got the most fulfilment from. So those are the ones to hunt out now. As with the values, aim to find 50 but a minimum of 25 – I promise you, you've got those. There's space at the end for you to add your own specific skills that aren't on this list.

Adapting to change	Building consensus
Analysis	Cheerleading
Budgeting	Client management

Communication

Computer literacy

Creating beautiful

presentations

Creativity

Critiquing

Customer service

Delegating

Design

Editing

Enthusing others

Following directions well

Idea generation

Influencing

Innovating

Intuition

Leadership

Listening

Maintaining accurate records

Managing difficult situations

Managing spreadsheets

Marketing

Mediating

Mentoring

Motivating a team

Negotiating

Networking

Organizing

Planning

Presenting

Problem solving

Project completion

Project management

Promoting

Questioning

Running meetings

Selling

Setting deadlines

Social media expertise

Speaking

Strategizing

Supervizing

Taking responsibility

Team work

Testing

Time management

Training others

Writing

_____

_____

_____

Now you've made a list of skills that you know you've got, let's think about the ones you might *want* to acquire. If you already know where you want your career to be heading then you should also be aware of the skills you might be missing in order to help you get there. However, if you're not quite so clear, think about three people you admire. What skills do they show that you'd like to have? Perhaps they're brilliant public speakers. Or maybe they are really calm in a crisis. Whatever it is, make a note below of these skills and start having a think about how you might acquire them (tip: asking the person you admire how they acquired them is a good first step).

_____

_____

_____

_____

_____

_____

A vision of the future

So now you've got an idea of the values and skills you might want to start focusing on within your career, we can now add another building brick in the shape of a vision. I'm not talking about the sort of vision where you're standing on the bow of a yacht somewhere in the Caribbean – although there is definitely a time and place for that sort of vision. We're talking here about a vision that is built on the bricks of your values and skills. There are two ways to do this, so let's start with the easy one first – the worst-case scenario.

Strangely enough, most of us find it easier to know what we absolutely don't want, rather than what we do want. So if you find it hard to articulate what you want, start with the opposite.

Imagine you are five years in the future. What is the worst-case scenario for your career? Is it that you're doing the same job now or that you have no job at all? Once you've got a scenario in your head (and you can repeat this exercise with a few different ones if it helps), ask yourself these questions about it:

- What makes this scenario so unpleasant?
- Who would be the worst sort of people for you to be working with?
- What would you be doing every day?
- What environment would you be working in?
- What would your schedule look like?
- What skills would be required from you?
- What would be the values of the company you would be working for?
- Which of your values would you be ignoring?

When you've got a good list take a look at it; you now know exactly what you don't want. We can now look at the second way to create a vision (the hardcore optimists amongst you might have gone straight to this option – I wish I had your joy for life!). If you know what you absolutely don't want, does that give you a clue as to what you *do* want? Reverse the answers you've got above and have a look; does that give you a good idea of what you would like in the future?

Parents – you might find that your vision for the future is heavily centred around your children. That's to be expected but make sure you find time for yourself in there too. For example, if you've decided that you want your child to go to university and your career planning is now being determined by earning enough to afford that, then that's an important goal. However, working yourself into the ground in a job you hate, purely so your child can go on to higher education, is a recipe for bad family relations. What if they decide they don't want to go? Or they go but hate it and end up resenting you for pushing them into it? You've just spent five years working towards creating a vision for someone else and that never ends well. So by all means factor them into your planning but don't revolve your life around theirs: that way many years of family therapy lie ahead.

Imagine you're five years in the future. What is the best-case scenario for your life? Get an image of where you are and what you're doing. Now answer these questions:

- Who are you with?
- What does your daily life look like?
- What do you do each day?
- What is the environment you live and work in like?
- Which skills are you using?

- Which of your values are you committed to?
- How does it feel to be in this life?

Now you've got your values, your skills and a vision, it's time to get really cheesy and write a vision statement – one or two sentences setting out who the 'future you' is and how they live their life. If you're struggling to write this, a simple formula is:

I am… and the impact I create is…

The first part of the sentence might be more about your values and the second more about your skills. Let me give you a couple of examples:

- I am a forthright, determined and honest leader, and the impact I create is that I motivate those around me and make sure the job gets done.
- I am a warm, hard-working and community-driven human who supports creativity from idea to fruition and brings exceptional examples of this to the wider world.
- I am an award-winning, driven and fun professional who brings depth, innovation and time to listen to all areas of my life.

These are jumping-off points, yours might be longer or shorter. More work-focused or more life-focused. And it will almost certainly take more than one draft – that's fine. Spend some time playing around with it until you find something that you feel a connection with. It doesn't have to be perfect but if you find you keep coming back to it, that's a good place to start.

Now think about how your life might look if you organized each day around that vision statement. If you put those values and skills into play in your life each day. What would you have to change? What would you need more of? And what would you need to say no to? Try filling out the following lines:

In order to have a life that meets my vision statement:

1. I need more _____.

2. I need to say no to _____.

3. The things I need to change are _____

_____.

From vision to action

So, you've got a vision and now you need to execute that vision. It's time for action and that action needs a strategy.

Strategy is what we mean when we talk about execution; it's moving from the 'what we want to do' to the 'how we're going to do it'. Think about it as though you are an army officer commanding your troops. Who are the people, and what are the processes, behaviours and targets you need to have in place in order to meet that vision? Once you have these in place, you have a roadmap for your career plan so take the time to make sure you have all the bases covered.

First off, let's start with some targets. If you were to break that vision down, what are some key things that need to happen in order for you to achieve it? There are going to be some things which *have* to happen and some things which you believe have to happen. See if you can spot the difference. For example, if you want to be the world's leading graphic designer you are definitely going to have to come up with some designs, in fact you might need a certain number or a certain level of skill to make you the world's 'leading' graphic designer. You might believe, however, that you have to work more hours than anyone else or that you have to be a certain gender or that you have to be taken seriously by your boss or that you have to only take on the biggest brands with the greatest chance of awards. None of these things are necessarily true.

The difference is that targets that *have* to happen are usually more under your control than the targets you *believe* have to happen. Any targets that revolve around other people's views of you are probably worth dismissing; you're looking for things you can influence not things that are ultimately out of your control. So in the above example, some useful targets might be:

- Work with X amount of companies to design their brand identity.
- Spend X hours a month researching and learning from industry leaders.
- Aim to enter your work into two awards.

Some less useful targets would be:

- Have my boss tell me I'm brilliant at my job.

- Work more hours than my colleagues.
- Never fail.

Can you see the difference? Great. Off you go and set some targets. If they're really big you might want to break them down, so you might have a one-year target and a five-year target, for example. Aim to set at least three targets you feel excited by.

1. _____

2. _____

3. _____

Once you've got these targets, it's time to break them down. Going back to the analogy of the army officer organizing their troops, now you've got your targets you have to think about what you need to do and who you need to help you hit them.

For each target, write the steps that need to happen in order to reach this. So, using the example above, it might look like this:

Do X number of rebrands in the next year:

1. Ensure that my boss knows I want to do X number this year and ask them what I need to do to make sure I can hit that target.

2. Find, and ask, a more senior designer to mentor me.

3. Book onto two professional development courses to ensure I have the most up-to-date skills.

Next to each of these write down the names of the people you need to talk to about this. Perhaps you need the human resources director to sign off on some professional development budget for you or you know someone you'd like to approach about mentoring. Get their names down here and next to those names write the date you are going to talk to them about this by. There is nothing like a deadline to get things done and if you don't put a date down, trust me, it's not going to happen. Even better, once you've got that date down make sure the action is marked in your diary and you've set a reminder about it.

Target	Steps to reach it	Who to speak to	Date
1.	_____	_____	_____
	_____	_____	_____
	_____	_____	_____
2.	_____	_____	_____
	_____	_____	_____
	_____	_____	_____
3.	_____	_____	_____
	_____	_____	_____
	_____	_____	_____

In order to achieve some of these targets you might need to change your behaviours or working patterns, so think about how you can do that. For example, if you know you're going to need quiet time to get research or professional development done, this might be worth looking into for the days when you're working from home. Equally, if you know that your boss is going to be more responsive to any requests you have for them at the beginning of the week, make sure you book that meeting or call in then. Use the planning you've done on your working patterns and boss management in the previous chapters to help you reach these targets and achieve your vision.

And now to get going

What you should have now is a clearly set-out vision and strategy, and a career plan you've built yourself that you're ready to inhabit. Have a look at what you've got here. What feels doable? What feels scary? What feels like it might never happen? Is there anything that feels impossible? Don't worry if there is, that's normal, you can get there. You might just have to start small. If it feels a bit overwhelming simply ask yourself, what's the first step that you're going to take to achieve this vision?

It might be setting up a meeting with your manager or a potential mentor. It might be signing up for some train-ing. You might want to sit down with your family and talk about what it means for all of you. It might be talking to your manager about a promotion. Once you've identified it, do that now. Go on, put the book down at this point and go off and do that first thing. Off you go.

Have you done it? Feel a sense of accomplishment? Good: hopefully that feeling is going to accompany you the whole way through this book and your career.

Making these plans happen on your own

So now you've got a plan, how do you put it into action? This will vary slightly depending on whether you work for yourself or as part of a wider company. We'll look at the latter in a minute but first I wanted to give a bit of a boost to those sole traders and freelancers out there making it happen for themselves.

When you work for yourself it can feel as though every minute counts and as though the most important thing you can do is bring in the money – and it is. But this often means we take work that doesn't fit our career aspirations and which we don't really enjoy. It also means that we often underprice ourselves as we're just so grateful to have the work. This leads to us being busy but unfulfilled and often stuck in the same place for years at a time until something forces us to make a change.

Consider this, that force. It is possible to have a career plan that requires you to focus on one area or even to pivot your business and still keep your clients happy and make money, but you just have to take it step by step. First up, ask yourself what you can say no to. Is there one job you could turn down to make time to move yourself further towards your goal? Could you bring in another freelancer to take some of the work off your hands in return for a fee that's lower than what you're charging the client, so you're both making money? Or can you sacrifice a client or money in order to devote time to making that shift? After all, if it works you should find that you don't actually lose out at all in the long run.

The second problem a lot of freelancers face is focus. We've decided we want to do something but life keeps getting in the way, and without a boss to keep us on track we're entirely responsible for our own motivation. It can be easy to give up early if things don't go exactly to plan first time or to move our attention onto something which seems like a quicker win. A way around this is to create a visual reminder of what you're working towards and stick it above your desk. It might be a picture of where you see yourself in five years or a slogan or phrase that absolutely sums up why you've created this plan for yourself. Whatever it is, make sure you can see it each day to give yourself a little shot of motivation.

And finally, what if you don't think you need a career plan at all? Life has been ticking along nicely for you, you've got some clients, you're making good money – why would you need to think long term? I thought like this for a long time but there comes a point when you realize that a lack of direction means that when things are good, they're good but the second a client drops out or the money becomes a little lean, you're in a place of panic. Having a plan can alleviate that fear – it shows you where you should be going and reminds you of the next steps you can take. So take some time to make that plan, in the long run you'll thank me.

Sharing your plans with your boss

For many of you employed in a company, one of the early steps you'll have to take is talking to your boss about your career ambitions. We often blame our manager for us not getting far enough in our careers. We think that they are somehow responsible for helping us but, as I mentioned in the previous chapter, the reality is that your manager is far more focused on their own career than they are on yours. Yes, I know, you think it should be the other way around, but no, they're really thinking about what they want to achieve and where they want to go. Because of this you'll probably end up with either a manager who hasn't given a second thought to your career development or one who assumes that their own ambitions are also what you want to be doing with your career. It's very human to assume that because we want something so does everyone else. In reality, this doesn't work and it's up to you to tell your manager who you are and what you want to do. If they're a good boss, and let's assume they are, they'll want this information as it means they'll be able to help you better.

So it's time to have a talk with them. What's the best way to do this? We're so used to doing this in person that, actually, it can be hard to think about how we do it if we're not in the office together. If both you and your manager work from home at different times or your office schedules don't cross over, you might find you have to do this virtually. So here are some simple tips for managing that.

First of all, block out longer than you think you're going to need. Most people block out an hour for a meeting, but in this case make sure you block out 1½ hours with your boss (if this seems like a lot you can start the meeting by saying 'I don't see this taking longer than an hour but I thought I'd give us a buffer' – that way you've just given them back 30 minutes of time which should start the meeting off on a good note). For you, make sure to block out 30 minutes before-hand so you've got time to prepare for it and 30 minutes afterwards so you can make notes and follow up on anything that's been agreed. This also means you won't be rushing from one meeting to another and you can go into this talk calmly and feeling prepared.

Secondly, think about the format you will feel most comfortable with. I prefer a video call because I think it's easier to know how people are responding to your ideas if you can see their body language. But if you know you're going to find it easier to do this via a phone call, or even an email, don't rule those options out. Particularly if you know your boss prefers those methods too. The advantage of both of these is that you can actually write yourself a script and nobody will see you reading it. Even if you do choose to do a video call, having some key points written on Post-its and stuck on your screen so you can see them as you talk is a good idea. It will make sure you don't forget anything important and help you keep the conversation on track.

Finally, when you're having this conversation, look and listen for some key prompts from your manager. Are they

leaning into their screen? That tends to be a signal of engagement (or that they can't hear what you're saying, so do check).
If you can't see them, are they repeating back phrases that
you've used? That's a good sign that they're listening prop-
erly, whereas if they take the conversation off on a completely
different tangent consider that a sign that you're probably
going to need to follow up with an email that repeats what
you want them to remember.

Signs that someone isn't listening or engaged in the
conversation might include: if you're on a video call, seeing
their eyes move around the screen (a clear sign someone is
reading emails while they're talking to you). You might see
them leaning back from the call. They might try to assert what
they want rather than what you want. They might give you
reasons for why it's not possible at the moment, or they might
even try to turn the session into a discussion about areas you
could improve on.

If your boss doesn't seem responsive don't spend lots of
time trying to convince them. Instead, ask them if there's
anything they'd like to feed back to you here about your
proposal? If not, follow it up in an email and then set a time
to talk to them about it again in the future. Remember, just
because you're engaged in forwarding your career doesn't
mean they will be, so you'll have to keep the pressure on.
I once worked with a man who asked his boss for a pay
rise every six weeks without fail. Did he get one every six
weeks? No. Did he get one more often than the rest of us?
Absolutely. Keep going.

And finally

What will become more and more apparent as you start working through your career plan is that you can't do it alone. You're going to need to bring in the reinforcements, particularly so if it starts to feel like your boss isn't on your side. If you're working from home this can feel particularly difficult. When you're on the second day in a row where the only company you have is a pot plant called Fred, all of us feel a bit alone in the world. The good news is that there is almost certainly company and inspiration somewhere on the internet, so you don't even need to leave your house to find it. Building your network, and helping them to help you, is possible no matter where you're working. And in the next chapter, I'll show you how.

Questions to think about

- **What do you now know your key values and skills to be and how will you use them to drive your career plan forward?**
- **What is the one action that you need to stop doing in order to move your career plan forward and how will you stop doing it?**
- **If your career plan works out as you hope it will, what will the reward of that be? What will your life look like and how will you be happier?**

CHAPTER FOUR

BUILDING YOUR NETWORK

'But I thought working from home meant I didn't have to spend any more time with my colleagues?' I hear you cry. 'I thought I could forgot all that schmoozing and office politics and instead just quietly get on with my job from the comfort of my sofa?'

I wish I could tell you that is true, but unfortunately it's not. If you want to progress your career, you are going to need a network of people to help you. You can't do it alone. We like to believe that we are promoted or hired purely on our performance and experience, but sadly that's not the case. Most of the time people will hire people that they like, people who are like them, or people who have been recommended to them. If you can find a way to create a connection with someone, to add them to your network, you might find that as you climb the career ladder they suddenly come in useful (or you might be able to help them climb their career ladder, which always gives a good-deed glow). To misquote Barbra Streisand in *Funny Girl*, 'People who need people are people with jobs.'

The first thing to realize when you are building a network is that it's not just about making friends with your boss or others further ahead on the journey who might be able to help you. Building a network means creating connections in all directions. I like to think of this as building up and building down. Just as we look to people for help and guidance, so should we be providing that help and guidance to other people – partly because it's a nice thing to do but also because you never know where they're going to end up! A lot of the work that I have picked up has come about because of the people that I helped when they were more junior. I might have helped to get them a job or given them some advice or some free mentoring and they've progressed in their career. And as they've progressed, there have come opportunities where actually, they can help me. They might be able to introduce me to people, offer me work, give me career advice. So when you're looking at building a network, you want to think about building up and building down. This is particularly important in a world where more of us work from home – those junior members of staff who might have learned on the job from those around them in the office, now need people to reach out and actively help them. Be that person.

Building down is particularly important amongst groups that are underrepresented in the workforce. For black, Asian or other racially marginalized groups, finding people at the

top of organizations who look like you can be all too difficult. That's not to say there won't be other people that you can
use to build your network up but it's also worth recognizing
that those coming into the workforce behind you will need
the support that you might have missed out on when you first
started. Having the support of other people potentially facing
some of the same biases and blockers can bolster you and them,
and help ensure that the numbers at the top start to change.

Don't discount the connections you make in other areas
of your life too. Parents have a built-in network through their
kids. The school gate has far more potential connections than
your office, and someone owing you for babysitting their
child at the last minute is pretty much a blank cheque when it
comes to future favours.

Building your network up

Building your network is essentially thinking, 'Where do I want
to be going in my career and who are the people that I need to
know in order to help me get there?' Don't worry if this feels like
a daunting task or if you feel as though you don't have the right
connections or background. When I started in journalism it felt
as though everybody either knew everybody else or was actually
related to them (sadly it stills feels that way a lot of the time and
I think it always will). I felt like the odd one out for years, until
I started to find other people lingering on the outside just like
me. We formed our own network and it turned out to be just as
strong. Just because you don't have a network of contacts from

your family, school or university, doesn't mean you can't create that network for yourself. The reality is that you might have to be a bit more proactive and daring than those who can just pick up the phone to someone they went to school with. The good news is that being proactive and daring are excellent life skills to acquire and will stand you in much better stead in the long run than having the right surname.

So, let's get going on creating that network. Think back to the past chapter where we did that career-mapping exercise, looking at what the goal and the strategy was. Within the strategy, there was a question about identifying the people needed to help you achieve that. Who did you put down? Were they all people you knew personally or were there some gaps? It doesn't matter if there were gaps; in fact that's great because it shows you where to focus on growing your network next. Just because you don't know someone now, doesn't mean you can't in the future.

When we're mapping out the people we need in our long-term strategy we're actually playing a game from childhood – Six Degrees of Kevin Bacon. The principle behind this game was that all of us were only six degrees of separation away from the Hollywood actor, Kevin Bacon. For example, if I wanted to meet Kevin Bacon and I was going to be really pushy about it, my six degrees of separation might look a bit like this:

1. My friend Emma is a location assistant for TV and film.
2. Her boss, Claire, has worked in the movie industry for over 30 years, with a range of actors and directors.

3. Claire might have worked on a film with Kevin
   Bacon and therefore might know him personally or,
   more likely…

4. Has worked with a producer who has worked with
   Kevin Bacon and knows him well.

5. Which would take me to Kevin Bacon.

Now I know there is a lot of presumption in there and absolutely no guarantee that any of those people would know
the right person to introduce me to, and no reason why any
of them should want to use their own connections to help
me…but they might! And along the way to potentially meeting Kevin Bacon I'd make new connections, learn about new
industries, understand more about other people, grow my
confidence in talking to new people, maybe be able to offer
up some of my own skills to help some of them, and generally
move myself and my career forward. Even if I never got to
Kevin Bacon, I'd still have gained an awful lot in the process.
And this is the thing to remember when building out your
network: it might not be a straight path from first connection
to end goal but the experience you'll gain along the way will
be worth the effort.

So, here's your first exercise for this chapter:

Look at some of the people you have named in your
strategy from the last chapter: who do you need to know, or
maybe need to create a better connection with there? Working
through the Six Degrees of Kevin Bacon, how could you get
there? Write these names down in the spaces below. They

might not be right. You might be taking a guess, that's absolutely fine. Just think about it as a detective novel; if you talk to enough people you'll eventually work out who holds the key to unlocking the mystery.

1st person to talk to			
2nd person to talk to			
3rd person to talk to			
4th person to talk to			
5th person to talk to			
6th person to talk to			
Your Kevin Bacon			

Give to get

One of the questions I hear a lot when I talk to people about networking is, 'Why would anyone want to talk to me?' This fear that we don't hold enough value to be worthy of our network is common but instead of asking, 'Why would they help me?', I suggest asking, 'How can I help them?' People always remember a favour and even if you're really junior, don't underestimate the ability you still have to help other people and raise your profile at the same time. Behold simple ways to grow your network and give back:

1. **Offer to mentor.** People are always looking for mentors. It sounds grand but essentially it's just a way to offer your experience to someone. This means mentoring can both build up and build down. Traditionally mentoring was senior to junior but more and more companies are offering reverse mentoring where junior staff advise senior staff on anything from digital strategy to diversity. Just because you're working from home doesn't mean you can't be a mentor. In fact, it's probably easier – a 30-minute Zoom call has replaced an hour's meeting. Plus, you can do it across the world. The Cherie Blair Foundation for Women teams up female mentors with economically disadvantaged women from developing countries. You can practise your mentoring skills, build a network through the other mentors and increase your knowledge and understanding of the world. Plus, you help a woman who needs it. One thing: I sometimes find someone asking me to mentor them stressful, if it feels like a never-ending agreement. If you are in a mentor role and feel the same, set up clear boundaries from the beginning. For example, mentoring lasts no more than three sessions and the mentee has to come with a clear plan for what they want to talk about each time. Do whatever you need to do to make it feel straightforward.

2. **Create a space for people from work to talk about things that aren't work.** This might be a Slack channel or a weekly Teams meeting where the only agenda is no

agenda. Post-2020 lockdown I think we're all over the online quiz but there's still demand for online events and talks that are actually useful or interesting for people. Be the person who decides to bring in an inspirational speaker once a month and you'll grow your network both internally and externally. N.B. If you're going for the really big-name speakers, you'll need a budget, but HR might be able to help you with that. And many speakers who would otherwise cost a fortune can be got for free when they've got a book to promote so keep an eye on the book charts and see who is looking to move their way up the bestseller list.

3. **Become an information resource.** This is a simple way to get yourself known without having to organize lots of events or spend lots of time with other people – really one for introverts. If you love reading and are signed up to all the news alerts and the best newsletters then once a week/ month/quarter do a round-up for people that don't have your brilliant research skills. You might want to set this up as an actual newsletter but you can also send it as an email – just be aware of keeping everyone's emails safe and private if you take it outside of your company. Whether you're doing this for an internal audience or industry-wide, make sure your personality comes across. We'll talk about personal brand in the next chapter but putting your stamp on this makes it more fun for readers and helps people connect with you as a person, rather than just another email.

4. **Finally, be a wise elder.** Think about the junior members
    of other teams that perhaps you've worked with but don't
    really know. If they're also working from home they're
    going to be in need of someone to help them understand
    the business better and also give them some help with
    their boss. Set up a virtual coffee, have a chat and just
    hear what their gripes are. Give them a space to moan and
    then give them some older, more experienced wisdom.
    New parents really need this support; being the person
    a new mum can check in with when she returns from
    maternity leave is one of the kindest things you can do.
    Remember that nobody is so unimportant that they don't
    deserve your time. Everyone feels better from a little
    attention and advice from somebody they admire. And in
    the long run, you never know where they'll end up.

Introverts and extroverts

One of the questions I get asked most about networking is:
'What happens if I'm an introvert who hates large gatherings
and cannot bear the idea of networking?' Since we've all been
working from home more, the flip of this has been: 'What
happens if I'm an extrovert and I simply cannot bear the idea
of having to build my network purely online?' Well, don't
worry. There are solutions for both of these.

For the introverts among us, networking feels like this vast,
overwhelming sea of people that we have to connect with and
impress. The good news is that if you just have a gentle one-to-

one chat with someone, that is also networking – it doesn't have to be a big thing. If you're working from home a lot, one of the advantages is that online networking works better with smaller groups. Peer-to-peer mentoring works really well and is brilliant for alleviating loneliness. And it doesn't have to be in person. Set up a WhatsApp group of supportive colleagues and friends and agree to celebrate each other's wins and boost each other up.

And if you really don't want to get too in-depth, we have social media. I do social media a disservice by suggesting it's lightweight. Some of the best relationships and business I have, have come from connections that I have created over social media. That means doing a little bit of (non-scary) stalking. You don't want to know everything about everyone, but finding out someone's interests, in advance of actually meeting them, can really help build a sense of friendship much more easily, particularly if you're meeting online.

Extroverts, this is not your idea of fun, I know – you want to actually see people! Soak up their energy! The idea of having to leave the party behind and stay at home and never see anyone in person again feels like a death to you. But don't worry, you can still work from home and build your network without feeling completely bereft. First thing is to think about who else in your vicinity is working from home. Can you work together sometimes? Could you go for a weekly walk together? Find a way to get that face-to-face time, even if you're not in the office.

Extroverts don't need people around them all the time but they do generally need someone to bounce ideas off. You might want an extrovert friend who is happy to have you pinging them messages or voice notes during the day, and will do the same for you. If you really like working with someone, suggest video calling them and have them on another screen, your phone or tablet, while the two of you work. It can be very soothing having someone working alongside you even if they're not physically there.

And if you want more face-to-face time, gather together a small group – six is great, 12 maximum – and once a month have an online call where you help each other with any work problems that have come up. These might be work colleagues or ex-colleagues but try to get a mix of people in and out of your business. Don't make yourself responsible for inviting everyone; invite a couple of your contacts and ask them to invite a contact. That way everyone meets someone new. Agree to keep all conversations confidential, set a date and make sure everyone gets equal time to talk. And voilà, you've set up a very neat and useful networking group.

Schmoozing the boss

Obviously the key reason for networking is so that you can move your way up the career ladder and one person who can definitely help or hinder that is your boss. We think that we need to influence our boss but really you need to think about influencing your boss, your boss' boss and your boss' boss' boss. Go at least three rungs up the chain, if you can.

Don't worry that this might offend your boss: just because you're getting on with their boss doesn't mean you're trying to oust them (it could but it's worth trying to disguise that in case it doesn't work!). Rather than networking behind your boss' back, do it in front of their face. Copy the Big Boss into a weekly update or note celebrating the completion of a project, but just make sure to praise your boss in the email. Even if they were no help at all. You look good. They look good. You've built a relationship with their boss. They can't complain about it because you bigged them up at the same time. It's a win-win.

Also think about in that email saying something like, 'If you want to talk about this further, I'd love to make some time for you or it'd be great to do a presentation to the team about it.' Never miss a chance to tell people what you're doing.

One thing to be aware of when you are building your network up is that management changes, and faster than you think. So don't just build a great relationship with your boss, try to build relationships with their colleagues too. If somebody is running a workshop or presentation, talking about a different department from yours, go along and at the end of it, drop them and the leader of their department an email to say how interesting it was and what you've learned. If you're working from home that day and it's not available to watch online, email them to say you've heard great things, can you have a video call or could they share the slides? Show interest and be positive, that's all you need to do to leave a good impression.

One of the really great things, actually, about working from home is that it gives us an excuse to send those emails. If you're in an office with someone it can feel a bit awkward to email somebody on the other side of the room just to praise their team. But if you're not in the office, you can say, 'I'm not here today, so I can't pop around to say it, but I just wanted to really acknowledge how well your team has done and what I've learned from them.'

What we're doing when we are working with our boss' peers is acknowledging the fact that our boss might leave one day. If that happens, you want to make sure that you still have enough connections within your company, that your job is safe and maybe they even support you progressing into your boss' role. All of this is networking. It doesn't feel like it, but it is.

And if it all feels a bit awkward...

Just a short note to anyone who feels really awkward at this point. If you've been brought up to believe that networking is akin to brown-nosing, this might all feel a bit creepy to you. But I like to look at it as actually, you just want people to think the best of you and themselves. Don't tell someone they've done a great job if they haven't but if they have, it's nice to spread a bit of positivity, so throw those compliments out as fast as Oprah hands out cars.

Of course you have to be authentic; if there is somebody in your organization or your industry that you just don't like, there is no point sucking up to them just to build a connection. But I would urge you to see if you can take the personal out of it. Maybe you don't like them but you can appreciate what they do? And if you really can't, then don't waste your time on it. Connections have to be authentic for you. Plus, people are naturally suspicious. If we feel like we're being brown-nosed or picked up because somebody else wants something from us, we tend to back away.

And if you still feel really uncomfortable about networking, then do it from the angle of my friend, creative agency founder Emma Sexton. Rather than making connections with people in order to find ways they can help you, make connections so that you can find ways to help them. Come to all networking with the question, 'How can I best help this person?' If you do that you'll find it much less awkward.

Networking from home

So how is networking different from home? Well, the first thing is that there are more opportunities. Yes, that's true. There are actually *more* opportunities networking from home. Think about it. Even if you spent the day sprinting around the city you work in, you'd probably max out at about three networking events. For parents balancing work with childcare and school runs, it's even less. Online you could attend ten different webinars if you wanted to. You could organize 16 different video calls and, as long as you keep to the point, you wouldn't even be late for any of them. There are actually more chances to meet more people when you're working from home, you just have to reach out to them.

As more people work from home, there are more people out there looking to make connections with people outside of their office. This means if you reach out to them, you'll probably get a positive response. We're all looking for people to interact with. So if you want to form a network for your industry or your company or the people who live locally to you, or any other group, now is the time to do it.

There are some difficulties of working from home when it comes to networking. It can be hard to build those spontaneous connections, those water-cooler moments that take someone from work colleague to friend. You have to work at it; you have to set up coffee video calls, you have to make sure you keep up your one-to-ones, you have to take the time to keep your boss updated, you have to reach out to new joiners and set up a time to connect with them, you have to follow up on that business card a client gave you and you stuck in a pocket and forgot about. In short, you have to be conscious about it.

Paid, earned and owned

I like to think of networking from home in the way that marketing managers now think about promotion. There is paid-for marketing (e.g. ads in the media), earned marketing (publicity gained through promotional efforts) and owned marketing (your own website or social media). Paid, earned and owned. And I think we should be looking at networking in the same way. Here's what I mean:

PAID NETWORKING

This is, unsurprisingly, when you pay for access to a group or individual. Over the past few years there has been a boom in online courses and paid-for membership sites, and a lot of these can be excellent value for money. While membership of an in-person club might set you back thousands, an online membership can be as little as £5 or $10 a month and provide many more opportunities to meet people. If you're going to pay you need to make sure you're going to get your money's worth so ask some questions first. If it's an online course make sure what you learn will practically improve your career, and ask how much access you'll have to the tutor and other participants. If you're looking to build your network as well as learn, it's worth paying a bit more and finding a course which has a regular coaching or accountability call. A lot also offer closed Facebook or WhatsApp groups that allow you to meet other members.

Online memberships can be a good investment because you already know that the members are interested in the same things you are, and are maybe working in a similar area. They should provide you with good opportunities to learn but also to participate – whether that's asking for advice in a closed forum or through smaller, more intimate events with sector experts. One of the things that is so valuable about online courses and memberships is that often we go to them with a level of vulnerability and openness that we wouldn't do in our professional 'working lives'. That makes for really strong bonds. And it's those bonds that you need as you go through your career.

EARNED NETWORKING

These are other people's networks that you join and help to grow. Within your own company this might be a network focused around gender, race or sexuality, or perhaps a team sport, book club or quiz group. Anything that is already running that you can contribute to counts here. You don't have to go as far as joining the organizing team, although that often offers great opportunity for skills development; simply championing the events they do within your own team, possibly writing a blog post for them afterwards or just talking about their work on social media helps. Actively encouraging and building up the people that have run those networks is a great way to build your network both up and down, and gives some often unsung heroes a little bit of recognition for a hard job.

OWNED NETWORKING

I think owned is the most interesting option here. Owned is about using your working from home time to also create your own active networks. It seems like a lot of work but you can start small and still have real impact. For example, a weekly video call which brings together cross-industry participants at a similar level – everyone gets two minutes to talk about what's going on for them and then three minutes to hear feedback/advice from the rest of the group. What about something even easier, like a Slack channel devoted to daily wins from your team – as big as a new client or as small as sending a difficult email. Ask yourself what would help you and go from there. Even if only a couple of people show up to begin with, you'll have started something and from there you only have to keep going.

One other idea which I love is a shared Spotify playlist which everyone working from home plays at the same time –

say a Friday afternoon – as it plays in the office. It puts you in a working mood but also gives you the feeling of being part of a group of people as everyone is listening together and can flag what they love (or hate) on a shared WhatsApp or Slack group.

Building connections online

The part of working from home that everyone seems to find hardest is building the depth of relationship that we seem to create effortlessly with colleagues when we are in an office with them all day, every day. When you see your colleagues for eight hours a day you quickly learn their quirks and moods. You know that if your boss passes on the offer of coffee first thing it's because they're worried about something in the calendar. Or if your colleague is worried about a meeting with their manager later, they're not going to be the most focused in a new-project meeting. We learn to read these moods and in doing so we learn when we have been a cause of the mood's existence and when in fact it had nothing to do with us whatsoever.

The problem with working from home, however, is that everything can start to feel very personal. You get a short email from a customer and assume the shortness is a symptom of their dissatisfaction, that the lack of ebullience is due to a failing on your part rather than that they might just be busy or they're zooming through email and don't have time for niceties. Likewise, we have a video chat with one of our colleagues and see their eyes darting around the screen as we're talking to them. We assume they're bored and looking for something else to focus on – unfortunately it's easy to see when someone is reading their emails during a video conference – but it's almost certainly nothing to do with you. The problem with working from home, however, is that it becomes difficult for us to believe this.

When we're on our own we can tend to make up stories about what is going on with other people. If we were in a building with them we might pull them aside after a meeting or take them for a coffee, but you can't do that when your office is your home. So how do you start to learn when a situation has arisen that you need to address and when it's simply your own mind playing tricks on you?

THE BEST AND WORST OF VIDEO CALLS

The ability to talk to clients, colleagues and teams in real time, even when you're not in the same room, has been the tech that revolutionized working from home. Suddenly you could be on the other side of the world but you could interact with, and see, people as though you were together. Video calls, it was decided, were the way that work was going and we had to get used to them. The problem is that it can be hard to understand, and be understood, on a video call. Even the most reserved of us give away how we're feeling through our body language and that can be much harder to gauge on a call.

If you've ever done any public-speaking coaching then you know that one of the first things they teach you is that the least important thing about your talk is what you say. Generally, when we watch someone speaking we'll take in as little as

5 per cent of the words they say. The rest of our attention is caught up in how they stand, the tone of their voice and the energy they give off. It's why so many speaking coaches focus on getting their clients to project confidence in their stance and tone, before they even begin to worry about the words they're saying. The same is true of a video call: what we say is less important than the energy we give off. Unfortunately, all sorts of things can come into play here – maybe there's a bad connection, maybe the way you've set up your screen means it looks as though you're far away and therefore not that engaged. Perhaps you've been dealing with difficult clients and a washing machine which has broken down, or you're completely distracted by the strange clanging sound coming from the dishwasher, so your colleagues might notice that something is wrong on the call but they won't know why. Here are some things to remember:

1. Video calls are a performance. I am normally a big believer in being yourself at work – trying to fake it till you make it is a short-term strategy that most of the people you work with will see straight through. However, if there is one place to bring in your acting skills it's on a video conference. There is something about the camera that simultaneously dulls us down and magnifies every flaw we have. Screens can highlight every emotion and thought, and we need to be aware of that when on a video conference.

2. Ask yourself, what emotion do you want to portray on that video call? If we know that every feeling we have is going to be caught on camera, then we need to start by getting in the right mood. In this, working from home can be a real bonus.

3. When you're in the office, you go from your desk to a meeting, back to your desk and repeat, maybe with a quick pop to the bathroom in the middle. But really there is no space to yourself to reset and gather your energy. When you're working from home you can do exactly this. You have a space to set yourself up for meetings and make sure you show up as your best self rather than as the self that has been stuck at a desk for seven hours and is counting the minutes until home-time.

4. Before each meeting, give yourself two or three minutes to 'warm up'. Think about being a boxer before a big match. They'll do some exercises to get their muscles warm, they'll think about what they want the outcome of that match to be and then as they walk into the ring, they'll play some music that gets them in the mood. By working from home, you've got the space to do this too! Give yourself some time to do some stretching so you're relaxed, get absolutely clear on what you want the outcome of this meeting to be as well as the energy you need to project to get that outcome, and then play some music that will get you going. Give it a try and see how it changes your meetings.

BE YOUR OWN DIRECTOR

Look for your light! A simple way of having more impact on your video calls is to ensure that everyone can see you. You know those annoying Instagram influencers who are always going on about good light? Well, they've got a point. Think about how you set yourself up for your calls so that people can actually see you and interact with you. If you're lucky/unlucky enough to have teenagers living in the house with you, ask them to do this for you. They worked out where the best light was years ago.

I'm not suggesting that you need to buy a ring-light and stick a filter on your camera (definitely don't go with the filter options provided by some video-conferencing services; they make everyone look like a make-up model from the 1980s) but do think about how you can organize your setup so that you look interested. Get it right and video conferences can actually be a way to create some of those surprise connections.

Remember how during the 2020 lockdown, politicians appearing on the news curated their backgrounds so they appeared to be sitting in a very fancy library with only the cream of the literary crop behind them? Well, that wasn't a completely stupid decision. While we might want to protect our privacy, video calls are a way to learn about each other and build our connections.

I recommend creating a video conferencing 'nook' in your house, where all video calls are taken. Partly because this saves you the trouble of wondering whether your background is 'conference-call safe' each time you log on, but also because it allows you to show a bit of your personal side. If you can find a spot with the cliched bookshelf behind you, go for it but it could even just be somewhere that shows off a picture you particularly like or that different coloured wall you're so proud of painting. We're looking for what are known in the dating world as 'hooks' – points that people can reference when they want to talk to you.

For example, at a weekly online writers' session I attend, the writing part of the call starts off with a 'cheers' as everyone lifts their mugs of tea to their cameras. I always notice the quirky mugs and make a mental note of the owners' names. When I see those names pop up in the chat I'm more likely to respond to them because I feel like I know them a little bit – even though all I know is that we have a similar taste in mugs.

Another time, when I was completing a freelance project, entirely remotely, for a company, I managed to build a relationship with one of the team based on the interior of her living room. I had noticed that in the back of her living room she appeared to have a unique chest of drawers. One day, when we were both a little early to a meeting, I asked her about it. She had a great story about finding it in a flea market and getting it home across the city on a bus. We passed a happy five minutes talking about ridiculously large items we'd tried to transport on buses. It gave us a chance to build a bond that otherwise wouldn't have been there.

WATCH YOUR (BODY) LANGUAGE

No matter how comfortable or not you feel on camera, you need to think about your body language and how you fit in the frame. Imagine if you were a director, looking through the lens of a camera at an actor on set. You'd want them to be clearly positioned within the frame, and you'd want to be able to see enough of them that you could read their body language as well as their facial expressions. Try to replicate this on your video calls. Most video conferencing will allow you to see yourself on the screen before you enter the meeting – take advantage of this. But if you set your nook up correctly, you should be able to turn your video straight on and be confident that you're well arranged.

Be aware that if you set your camera screen to be a close-up everyone is going to be able to see every expression you make. You're better off aiming for an angle that captures head, shoulders and torso. Basically what you'd see of someone if they were sitting across a table from you.

LESS TIME, MORE FOCUS

We're going to talk more about meeting timings later in the book but for now I want to emphasize the importance of focus when it comes to video conferencing. Let me be blunt here: we know when you're reading your emails during a call. You might think you're doing it subtly and it might only be for a moment but it's been spotted.

This is of less importance when the meeting is full of people and you have some cover – although I will add that when you're running a meeting and you notice one person not paying attention, they're the person you remember. However, if it's a small group then you absolutely have to pay attention. You wouldn't check your phone halfway through a coffee date, would you? Okay, maybe you would but I'd be unimpressed if you did.

The difficulty with this total level of focus on a video call is that it's very tiring. When we meet people in real life we don't concentrate on them as much as we do when we see them on a video call, so less is more. Make those meetings shorter, aim for 30-minute catch-ups rather than an hour, and give your eyes a rest in between.

READING THE OPPOSITION

Let's look at this from the other side. How do you know if people want to engage with you and what can you do to build those connections when you're not literally face to face?

Just as we talked about your body language on a call, so you can read other people's. If you can only see their face then it will be clear when they are paying attention or not. But there are some more subtle cues to look out for too. Someone moving around a lot or flicking through their notes? They might just be desperate for the bathroom but they also might have a point they want to make or an idea to share. Or they might also really disagree with the point you've just made – so call them out on it. Ask them if there's anything they want to share or say you've noticed that it seems like they have something on their mind.

ASK DIRECT QUESTIONS

As a society we fear direct questions far too much and there is no greater need for them than when we're working remotely. That space leaves a lot of room for misinterpretation and doubt. If you're going to work remotely for a long period of time, you're going to have to become adept at asking the questions you don't want to ask.

Our desire to not ask the awkward question, to assume the problem is with us rather than the other person's mood or internet connection, drives a lot of unnecessary worry and doubt amongst home workers so commit now to not letting it happen to you. Email people after calls and ask how that call was for them or if there's anything else they need to talk about. Tell them you noticed that they seemed a bit distracted and ask if there's anything they want to talk about. And if they come back and tell you nothing is wrong, believe them. If it's not the case, it's on them to talk about it, you're too busy to second guess them.

DON'T FEAR THE SILENCE

One final thing to watch out for, or more accurately listen out for, is silence. If you don't know if you're more extrovert or introvert, ask yourself how you are with silence. If you find yourself leaping in to fill even a second's silence, then you're almost certainly an extrovert. On a video call a silence can feel particularly unnerving.

One way of getting around this is to define who is running the meeting – then they're responsible for filling the awkward silence! If you're the host, it can be easier to encourage questions in the online chat to avoid this happening. But if it's not your meeting and the silence descends, you can do your bit to help out. If it's an online event or talk, for example, the host might ask for audience questions and there's often an awkward pause while people wait for someone else to speak first. If you're a participant I really encourage you to put your hand up first and ask the stupid question. Trust me, if it's something you're wondering about then other people are wondering too and they will all be incredibly relieved that you asked it before they had to.

However, you can learn a lot from silence. If you're on a video call with lots of people and a question is met with silence, watch the faces of everyone else on the call. You'll probably see lots of people smiling awkwardly and waiting for someone else to speak but you might spot someone who clearly has something to say but is unsure of whether to do so. You can use the pause in the proceedings to pick up information about what the people on the call really feel, so use that knowledge to encourage that person to speak up by drawing them into the discussion in a friendly way: 'I think that sounds interesting – what do you think, Mia?'

The art of email

For most of us the main medium for work – regardless of whether you're in an office or at home – is email. While newer tech has popped up, most of us still run our working lives through email or something similar to it. So how can we use our written communications to build connections with other people?

Here are some dos and don'ts of managing your email while you're working from home. I will say this section falls heavily under the banner of 'Do as I say, not as I do' – I have yet to truly gain control of my inbox, due more to my own dislike of it than any overflow of emails, but if you can commit to even just one of these tips, you'll start to see new people coming into your network.

1. **If in doubt, send the email.** Is there someone you really want to connect with? Did you talk to someone at an event and you'd like to keep the connection going? Have you met someone who you think would be a brilliant mentor but you can't work up the courage to contact them? Email is the way to do it. The simple fact about sending an email to a new connection when building your network is that the thought of sending it is far scarier than anything that will happen after that. Perhaps they email straight back and you'll be able to set up a meeting with them. Or perhaps they never reply and you won't know if it's because you said something that upset them or because they weren't interested. In both situations their response says far less about you and much more about them. If they replied positively it's because you're giving them something they want – whether that's another connection for their network or the chance to

feel good about themselves by helping someone. If they don't reply, it's NOT because you are a terrible human being who took over their inbox and absolutely doesn't deserve to be replied to. It's probably because they're busy. Or an arsehole. Or both. Send the email. (N.B. This does not apply to ex-romantic partners. In that case don't send the email. You're welcome.)

2. **Assume the best.** Have you ever sent a quick email only to receive a reply wondering why you're being so difficult? Or have you ever received an email and wondered what you'd done to upset the person sending it? You ask and it turns out they think you're great and can't understand why you'd think otherwise. The point is, it's hard to read tone on email. Unless you know the person very, very well, it's much better to just take the position of when in doubt, assume they're well meaning. This a) saves you from having to worry about what you've done and b) makes it much more likely that you'll send a positive note back which will improve both of your days. Remember, tone is hard so assume the best.

3. **Connections build connections.** One of the best emails you can send is the sort of email that links up two people who previously haven't known each other but could be useful to each other. This is also the best kind of network building. When you do this, you help someone else build their network, you encourage them to do the same to

you and you make not one, but two people's lives better. So often we think networking is about going out there and seeing people yourself, but the reality is that the best networking is where you help someone out. Email is a brilliant way to do this. You don't have to organize everyone's diaries, you don't have to get involved beyond the initial intro. If you made one of these introductions a month, you'd start to see your own network growing. Make one a week and you'll know everyone you need to know within a year. Kindness breeds kindness, so offer up your own contacts and see who you get back in return.

A final note on email. It is never too late to reply to an email. Okay, it might be too late but the act of replying is better done late than never. So, if you're looking at an email in your inbox and feeling bad that you never got back to them, do it now.

The art of social media

We can't talk about networking from home without mentioning social media. For a lot of remote workers, social media is their link to the outside world and their water-cooler moment from home. It is also a powerful tool for building your network, when used right.

Rather than look at all the different types of social media you could be using, I think it's more useful to concentrate on the rules that apply across all of them and how you can use them to grow your profile. Social media platforms come and go but beneath them lie the basic rules of engagement that can help you develop a network.

1. Be yourself. Much as I would urge you not to use a filter on a video call, so I would urge you not to curate your life to look like someone else's. There is a difference between setting boundaries around what you share on social media and setting out a completely unrealistic vision of your life. If you largely spend your weekends walking the dog and watching box sets, then far better that your social media reflects that than suggests you're a book-mad fashionista.

2. However you use it, all social media reflects on your working life. Remember the days when we would put 'views own not my employer's' in our bios and that was good enough? Not any more. A general rule to adhere to on social media is: if you wouldn't say it out loud, while standing on your desk in the middle of the office, with your boss and the entire executive committee watching, then don't say it online. Even if you have a private profile. I don't care if your follower count is five and your privacy settings are set to maximum, save it for your WhatsApp groups (just make sure there's no one from work in there too).

3. Social media is inherently part of your career. Even if you work in a field where it seems unlikely social media

will ever play a part, it's still a part of your working life. For example, if you work in an obscure part of dishwasher engineering, the actual work you're doing might not garner much engagement but you as a person can still do so. You might interact with other people you work with on Instagram. Or you might add someone you met at a networking event to your LinkedIn. Or you might share an interesting piece of dishwasher engineering research on your Twitter. Or if you wanted true dishwasher-engineer celebrity status, you might do a series of videos on TikTok showing how to fix classic dishwasher problems, set to a backing track of a classic 1970s song. Just because no one is sponsoring you to do these things doesn't mean they're not part of your job and contributing to your career.

Making friends and influencing people on social media

So now you know the rules, it's time to take some action. Social media responds to the same strategy that you would take with any other part of your career. Work out what you want to achieve with it, work out what you need to do each week in order to achieve that, find anyone you need to help you, get on and do it. Simple, right?

No? Okay, let's break it down.

You've decided you want to move to the next level of your career. To do this you need to be seen as someone with experience and expertise on a certain subject, you need to build connections either within your own company or in other companies where you might be looking for a job, and you need to be first in line with recruiters when those jobs come up. Here's how a social media plan for that might look:

Goal: Find my next job within three months.

First steps:

1. Build up recognition within my industry – follow ten people per week working in roles or companies I would like to work with.
2. Share three thought-leadership pieces a week.
3. Write one response to one of these pieces each week and publish (you might use LinkedIn or Medium for this). Share on all my social media channels.

Next steps:

1. Reach out to recruiters and share my social media handles so they can get a feel for the sort of work I'm interested in.
2. Reach out to anyone in my network who might work for or with a potential employer. Ask them what it's like working there, about the company values and how they recruit.
3. Start commenting and engaging with industry leaders on social media. Share their work, ask them questions and generally get them used to seeing my name.

4. Use more 'personal' social media (remember no social media is truly personal) to reconnect with former colleagues and friends who might be useful in my job hunt.

Further actions:

1. Create a weekly social media action that engages other people in my profession – for example, ask people to share their learning or win of the week.

2. Ask for help in my career development.

You don't have to share that you're looking for a new job but ask others on social media for their career advice or one thing they think every aspiring person in your position should learn. Remember, people love to help.

If you followed this plan religiously for three months, you'd almost certainly have a new job at the end of it and you'd definitely have grown your network and have significantly more connections than you started out with. Consistency is key on social media but it can also be hard so make sure you a) plan out time to dedicate to it and stick to it. And b) bribe yourself with a reward at the end. One blog post written equals one glass of wine. It makes the whole thing much easier!

So now you know how you're going to grow your network, it's time to think about how you put your best foot forward and make sure they can't wait to engage with you. It's time to brag your way to the top!

Exercises to help you grow your network

Before you go any further make sure you've filled in the Six Degrees of Kevin Bacon exercise. Who do you want to reach and how will you get there?

Create a social media plan for yourself. Ask yourself the following questions:

- Which platforms do I want to concentrate on and why?
- How much time a week can I commit to them?
- How many people will I interact with each week and how?
- What one action will I do each week to engage people?

CHAPTER FIVE

BUILDING YOUR BRAND

Chapter Four was all about building up your network and once you've got that established, the question is: what do you want the people in your network to know about you? This is the part where how you show up and what you tell people about yourself starts to set the agenda for how your career pans out. Because no matter how well we think we're doing in our job, it's really other people's views and opinions that will get us that promotion or help us make that career change.

This is absolutely not to say that you have to decide that from now on you're going to show Glenn Close levels of boss-bitch energy. But it does mean that you have to take some responsibility for how people see you. The days of saying, 'Well, they just don't understand my style' are over; it's now your job to make sure everyone is clear on who you are and what you stand for. And if you're working from home, you're going to have to do all of this without actually being in their presence. But you should know by now that that is completely doable, right? Right!

We're about to dive into the murky world of what is officially known as 'personal brand' – yes, I hate this term as much as you do and find it horrendously cheesy and uncomfortable. It just conjures up images of Instagram influencers, trying to flog online courses and not giving you very much in return. That's not what we're talking about here. And so far, no one has successfully rebranded 'personal brand' so we're going to have to stick with it for now.

A quick side note, first: establishing your personal brand and having everyone understand who you are is not the same as having everyone like who you are. It is impossible to be liked by everyone and in the long term attempting that is only going to end badly. Rather than aiming for everyone else to like you, identify the people you need to respect you and work on them instead.

And now that we've got that clear, let's look at how you create your personal brand (yuck).

Identifying your personal brand

Do you know what people say about you when you're not in the room? Because that is your personal brand. What this essentially boils down to are the key values that you choose to show at work every single day. So, if you turn up to every meeting absolutely on time every day, and each piece of work is delivered ahead of time, part of your personal brand might be that you're very conscientious and punctual. On the other side, if you're someone who likes to speak up in meetings and is the first to order drinks at the bar on a Friday, your personal brand is probably more along the lines of a confident extrovert (or a very loud boozehound, depending on how long you're out drinking for).

OTHER PEOPLE'S OPINIONS

One key thing to note about your personal brand is that you're not entirely in control of it. That is to say, you might be speaking up in a meeting because you're confident in the subject, you want to make sure the best possible work is done and you're happy communicating information, and the other people in the meeting might think you're speaking up because you're a show-off. This is a problem that affects women and people from racially marginalized communities the most. There are already so many assumptions about how we should behave out there that when we challenge these assumptions people tend to take it badly. This is what's known as other people sometimes being asshats.

Unfortunately, you can't really get around this. But what you can do is a) like yourself enough that it doesn't matter and b) make sure that as much as possible you're sticking true to your values. What I mean by that is that if you show up with the value of openness, and that value translates into calling it out when there seems to be a big old elephant in the meeting, then that's okay. If everyone in that meeting takes it the wrong way that's more on them than on you. One way to smooth this situation is to tell people what your values are from the get-go, for example: 'I'm the sort of person who thinks it's really important to make sure we talk about the stuff that otherwise might go unsaid.' Generally, when we forewarn people of our values they're not then surprised when we show them and tend to react slightly more positively.

The other thing to note is that if you seem to be perpetually rubbing people up the wrong way then you might want to take a closer look at what is going on here. Often if our personal values jar with the people around us it's a sign that it might be time to look for a different job. And if we keep running into problems, regardless of the business we're in or the people we're working with, then it's time for some serious introspection. You might think you're trying to come across as someone with high standards but are you really just coming across as someone who is highly critical? This is the moment to call in a good friend and ask for some honest feedback. And then listen to it.

FINDING YOUR PERSONAL BRAND

So, now we've got the 'What is a personal brand?' out of the way, let's look at how we identify our own. There are three stages to this: past, present and future.

Past: This is the bit where you look back at the experiences and feedback you've had during your life and start to pick out the bits you want to keep and the bits you want to leave behind.

There are parts of our personality, and therefore our personal brand, that have been with us since we were children and now is the time to start noting down what they are. Think back to the feedback you were given as a child, what did friends and family say about you? For some people this can be a bit painful and if it is for you, then know you're not alone. All feedback tells as much, if not more, about the person giving it as it does us, but it can still have some use.

For example, as a child I received two pieces of feedback constantly. The first was that I had an old head on young shoulders and the second was that I was too opinionated – this one largely came from my teachers. As an adult both of these pieces of feedback make up part of my personal brand; the old head on young shoulders has been adapted – now the shoulders aren't so young – into bringing a thoughtful perspective to problems. And I've kept being opinionated just as it is, because I like it!

Obviously, there are other bits of feedback that I've received in the past that aren't part of my personal brand. I don't put out there that I can be very shy or that attention to detail is not my strength. We all have layers to us; the key with personal brand is to think about which ones you want to show to your professional world.

Present: Now have a think about what people say about you in the here and now. You might already have this feedback if your company performs regular 360-degree assessments but if you work for yourself or for a smaller business, then there's no reason why you can't perform your own 360-degree assessment. Ask clients, colleagues and trusted friends for some honest feedback, and then take an afternoon to assess what they have to say. A 360 asks for feedback from someone more senior than you, someone at the same level and some- one more junior. So you get to see yourself from all sides. Look for the areas where they overlap, these are the points of your personal brand that really shine through at the moment. Do you like them? And most importantly, do they fit where you want to get to in the future?

Future: Finally, think about your personal brand from here on. Who do you want to be and what would people say about you if you became that person? If you're working for a business that you want to progress in, it can be useful to have a look at the senior management and see if they have skills or values that overlap with yours. If so, these are skills and values that the organization seems to like so you might want to dial these up and make sure everyone knows that you share them. If, however, you want to be showing skills or values completely different to what you're doing now, then think about how you're going to have to shift people's perceptions of you.

Here is a hard and horrible truth: if you're currently doing a job you hate it's because you gave someone the impression that you would be good at it. If they hadn't believed your brand fit the job, you wouldn't be in this situation now. So make sure in the future that your brand fits the sort of work you definitely want to have. Or have an honest conversation with yourself about whether or not you're in the right career. If you keep finding that your job doesn't match your values, you might need to rethink your line of work. It's not enough to be good at your job, you need to enjoy it as well.

We'll talk about this more in a little bit but it's very easy for us to get stuck in a habit of doing work that we're good at but we don't necessarily like. We get a reputation for being good at something and so people give us more of it to do. Often we feel proud that we're good at it and so we take on more, so we can keep that feeling of importance, but we don't love it, we haven't chosen it and if we're honest it's not what we want to do in our career. If you find you're bored or frustrated with your current job, look at how much you're doing that you really enjoy and how much you're doing simply because you're good at it.

CHANGING YOUR PERSONAL BRAND

The good news is, if your personal brand keeps bringing you work that you don't really want, it's very easy to change it. Let me tell you a story. I once worked with a man who from the day he arrived in his job, told everyone he'd been hired by the company to be a strategist. At each of his introductory meetings he'd say, 'Hi, my name's Ollie, and I do strategy.' Whenever he met a new client, he'd introduce himself with 'Hi, I'm Ollie and I do strategy.' And so of course, all the strategic work that needed doing went to him. (And if you've ever worked in a team with a strategist you'll know it's basically the best job because you just tell people what to do rather than do any of it yourself.)

A few years later, when I was thinking about changing jobs, I went to Ollie and asked him how he'd been hired to do a job which solely focused on strategy. Turns out he hadn't been. In reality, Ollie had been hired to do a job very similar to the one I was doing at the time but he'd realized that he didn't want to be involved in the day-to-day running of projects, he wanted to be setting up the process and leaving it there. So he simply told everyone that was what he did – he was the strategy guy. And so people went to him for the strategy work, and nothing else. It was that simple.

Now, when he explained this to me, I was mildly annoyed that a) he'd got out of doing the boring parts of our job and b) that I hadn't thought of this approach first. But he taught me a really important lesson – tell people what you want and that is what they will give you.

Finally, know that as you go through your career and your life, parts of your personal brand will change. Big life upheavals tend to alter who we are and what we believe, so it would be strange if you decided on your personal brand now and never adapted it again.

The obvious example of this is if you choose to have children. You might think you know exactly who you are before you have children and then find, for example, that they soften you or toughen you up, or force you to become more organized or completely change your priorities. I think a sign of a great leader is someone who can admit that their experiences have changed them and communicate how they're now different. Traditional working culture has forced mothers in particular to keep silent about these changes, to pretend they popped out a baby and then skipped back to work as though nothing had happened. However, as more of us work from home – and as we see more of the home lives of those we work with – I think we'll be able to be more open about how our experiences shape who we are.

Learning how to brag

Before we look at implementing your personal brand, there are two things that I need to talk about. One is the instinctive shiver of revulsion that comes with the phrase personal brand and the other is the horror that most of us have around the concept of bragging.

On the first point, look, I know I've talked about how cheesy it is to have a personal brand but whether you want to have one or not, people will create one for you so you might as well get in front of it and actually set it for yourself. Get over the cheese factor and embrace it already.

The second thing is that having a personal brand can feel a bit like bragging. It can feel like you're saying, 'I am so excellent at this particular thing, you should always put me forward for it.' And is that such a bad thing? After all, if you do want to be hired to do a particular job your chance of that happening is increased if you're good at it, and increased again if people know you're good at it.

If you find it particularly difficult to admit that you're good at something, ask someone to do it for you. We can all have

a crisis of confidence – new mothers returning from maternity leave particularly – so sometimes we need to bring in a
cheerleader. Ask your best friend to write down all the things
they think you're brilliant at, as though you were saying them.
You should end up with a heartwarming list of things you're
good at and which you can repeat. Just make sure that they fit
with your personal brand and where you want to go in your
career. It's great that your friend thinks you're funny but if
you're shooting to be a judge, you might want to focus on the
point where they talk about how good you are at settling arguments. Once you've got a list you feel happy with, it's time to
start practising. Try it out each day in front of the mirror. You
should have some first-person sayings that go along these lines:

- 'Hi, I'm Harriet. I'm really good at writing.'
- 'Hi, I'm Harriet and I find it easy to help people analyse
  their career patterns.'
- 'Hi, I'm Harriet and when I talk, people listen.'

Obviously, it was mortifying for me to write the above out but
the more I do it, the more I start to believe that it might be
true, and I might be able to do the big things I really want to.
Just remember, you don't want to miss a chance to get your
dream job. And if you meet someone who might be able to
help you get it, but you can't tell them why you'd be good at
it, you'll miss out.

When it comes to bragging there is one way to do it and
that is to make the person you're bragging to feel as though they

were so lucky to hear all about you. Have you ever listened to somebody when they tell you what they're passionate about? When someone tells you about the one thing that really brings them joy and because they love it and have invested time in it, they've actually got really good at it, it's magical. Listen to an Olympian being interviewed about their sport and their place in it and you'll probably be so inspired you instantly hit the gym. Well, all of us have the ability to do that, we just have to talk about the things that *we love and are good at.*

In the classic leadership book, *The Big Leap*, Gay Hendricks talks about how most of the time we can divide our working life into four categories. The first category is things you love and are good at. The second category is things you are good at but if you're honest, you don't enjoy that much. The third category is things you love but are not very good at. And the fourth category is things you don't love and you're not good at. I always find it funny that everyone has something in the fourth category we do on a regular basis for our job; even though we're not good at it and we don't enjoy it, we somehow keep doing it. What Gay Hendricks suggests is that actually most of us should be spending the majority of our time in the box where we are doing things *we love and are good at.*

This is not to say that you will never again have anything on your to-do list that you don't enjoy or that you find a bit boring. But if you were spending the large majority of your time, and by that, I'm talking about 80 per cent of the time, doing the things you love and are good at, two things would happen. One, you would absolutely shine and people would be intrigued and want to know more about it because when someone talks about something they love and are good at, we feel their energy. We feel excited by it and attracted to it – when we're having fun at work people pick up on it. The second thing that would happen is that actually you would feel more fulfilled, more interested and be more excited by your own job, because you would be working in the space where you do your work best.

So, let's map it out. Divide a piece of paper into four sections: one for the things you love and are good at, one for the things you love but aren't good at, one for the things you're good at but don't really love and one for the things you're not good at and don't enjoy. Now in each of those sections map out first your current working life and then your dream working life. What would those sections look like if you were doing exactly what you wanted? Take a good look at the box that contains the things you love and are good at – those are the things you're going to brag about, that will become part of your personal brand.

Things you love and are good at	Things you love but are not very good at

Things you are good at but don't love	Things you neither love nor are good at

So now you've got a good idea of your personal brand, let's have a look at how you convey that to people no matter where you are in the world.

Treat yourself like a brand

Every big brand will have what is called its brand guidelines. These apply to how the brand markets itself across every channel – everything from email signatures to huge advertising campaigns. Do the same for your personal brand and you'll find you get labelled with the one value that inspires confidence from nearly everyone: consistency. The fantastically 1980s interpretation of personal brand saw it very much as what you wear, how you did your make-up and just how much power-suited dominance you could bring to a situation. It was very much about how you showed up in person. But here in the 21st century, thankfully without a power suit in sight, personal brand can be much more nuanced and often as much about what you don't say as what you do. Here are some simple ways to put across your personal brand even if you're not in the office.

Email: I've said it before and I will definitely say it again during this book – tone is hard to read on email. That said, if you can maintain a consistent tone people will quickly be able to understand what you mean. We've been brought up with some rules around emails such as keep them brief and make a point of signing off personally but if that isn't you, that's okay. Be florid with your language if it feels right to you and never again put your name at the bottom of an email if it feels pointless. But do stay consistent. If you always sign off and then one day don't, your team is likely to read that as pissed off.

Think about how your email signature represents you. Remember around about 2010 when everyone with an iPhone signed off their emails 'Apologies for typos, sending this from my iPhone'? The number one thing that sign-off conveyed was not that the sender cared about typos but they did really care about you knowing they had an iPhone. You might want to put links to your work or your social media profiles. If you work hours that don't meet the standard nine-to-five or you deal with countries in different time zones, you might want to set out the hours that you will respond to emails. When we're not in the office with people, they can't see our working patterns. If you were sitting side by side, a colleague would know what time you started or finished work, so wouldn't expect emails to be answered outside that time (hopefully), but if people can't see you, you're going to have to be more explicit in how you communicate with them.

Right now one of the most interesting things to notice in someone's email signature is whether they put their preferred pronouns. And if they do, is that a decision made by them or company policy? Whatever you decide with your email signature, see it as a space to convey a bit of who you are and how you see the world, along with any boundaries people need to know about if they're going to work with you.

Social media: You cannot be too clear about who you are and what your priorities are on social media. Most people coming to your profile will be doing so with only a modicum of knowledge of who you are and what you stand for. Remember that all social media is professional, even the stuff you think of as personal and private. I'm a fan of a bio which expresses what you do AND how you do it in terms of both skills and values. But there are other ways to express your personal brand through social media beyond just your bio.

If you use social media to share ideas and knowledge, then this is the perfect place for you to set out your stall on what you believe and how you like to work. Believe in the power of collaboration over competition? Then sharing articles giving ideas on how to do this better or promoting the work of leading thinkers in this field instantly shows where your heart lies. However, I would urge you to go further than this. Don't just share the article, also explain what resonated for you within it and ask others for their feedback.

This is a double-whammy – you're showing off your personal brand and also inviting others to come and debate with you, building your network as you do.

Social media can be a great place to share visually how you see the world. You don't have to be the world's best photographer to do this, simply thinking about the colours you use can change how people see you. Instagram covered in millennial pink? We know your age, the group you associate yourself with and probably could take a guess at your views on politics and culture. We might not be right but people are definitely reading more into the filter you've chosen to use than you'd realize.

Keeping your social media professional doesn't mean you have to wipe out all trace of your life outside of work. It's okay to talk about your children or hobbies but try to keep a ratio of 80 to 20 per cent professional to personal. Working parents, I'm afraid this particularly applies to you. It's tempting to see social media as a way of keeping friends and family up to date but I'd suggest using WhatsApp for that instead. There is nothing wrong with talking about your family on social media but do you really want everyone in the office knowing that your kid has decided to stop sleeping through the night or that potty training is a nightmare? Stick to the golden rule: if you wouldn't say it in front of your boss' boss, don't say it on social media.

Video calls: I talked in the previous chapter about creating a nook for your video calls and you can definitely use this to show your personal brand. Think of it as the 21st-century equivalent of picking your 1980s power suit. Be aware of what is visible in this nook – do you have pictures up or books on display? What do they say about you? I'm not saying you want to create the perfect vignette of a perfect life – instead show some character and tell people who you are, that's much more interesting.

Thinking about how you appear in those calls also goes beyond just what you wear and the body language you convey. Make sure that your values are being shown in your behaviour during the call. Want to be seen as visionary leader? Make sure you speak up, bring new ideas to the table and champion other people's ideas too. Want to be seen as a manager who gets the best from their team? Make sure you bring something to celebrate your team for to each call. Think about the one or two things you can do during calls to show off who you are and what you believe in.

It's normal to worry that you'll become a cliche of yourself, and you might! I worked with one woman who was so known for bragging about her team that the second she started saying, 'Let me just quickly tell you the one thing my team have done this week', everyone in the meeting would roll their eyes at her. But her team adored her and when the boss was looking for someone to motivate a department which was falling behind she was the first pick. Sometimes it might seem as though your values don't align with the theme of the day but keep living and breathing them and you'll find the right place for yourself.

Being your own PR agent

Now that you know who you are and where you want to go, it's time to put yourself out there in the public world. I'm not suggesting that you need to become the company's official spokesperson but there are lots of ways you can get yourself noticed within your industry while you're working from home.

Awards: Every industry has its own awards industry within it. Whatever you do and however you do it, there is an award for you out there somewhere. And with awards come a) glory for your current company and b) the chance to promote yourself to another company. So it's time to get applying.

A few things to note when applying for awards. Be as detailed as you can, don't just say you contributed to growing the company's annual turnover, say how much you contributed. Don't just say you mentor others in the industry, say how many people you've mentored and what they've gone on to do because of you. You want as many interesting facts about yourself in the entry as you can fit in the word count. And read the submission guidelines carefully; if they say they want to know about the last three years of work and you only give them two, you've just put yourself to the bottom of the pile.

Some awards make their money by charging people to enter. Often your business will pay for this so take it to your boss and the marketing team and see what they say. If they won't pay but it's a prestigious award and you think you're in with a good chance of winning it, and you can afford it, I would recommend applying anyway because…

Journalists: …love an awards list. Often when looking for new names in a particular industry they'll turn to awards lists. They're particularly likely to do this when looking for people from a specific group to talk to – if they realize they've written an article only quoting white men, for example, they're definitely Googling 'Black British Businessperson of the Year', so it's worth trying to get on the list if you meet the requirements.

It's worth trying to make friends with a few journalists anyway, particularly B2B journalists (these are the people that write for your industry magazines and websites). B2B journos are often looked down upon by consumer newspaper and magazine journalists (for no reason other than some sort of journalism hierarchy) so tend to appreciate being appreciated. Sharing a story they've written on your social media with praise for it, commenting on their posts or even just sending them an email with a 'love what you're doing' message, can be the doorway to a journo friend and some useful coverage. However, no matter how friendly you get with them, remember that for you they are a way to promote your personal brand. So tell them about the things you're interested in and would want to talk about. Ask to see any quotes before they're printed (not always allowed but as long as it's not controversial they should say yes) and make sure they chime with how you want to be seen in your industry. It's really not true that all publicity is good public-ity, but publicity which promotes your personal brand can sometimes be very useful.

Speaking: For those of you who choose to work from home because you prefer your own space, this might not be for you but when it comes to promoting your own career there is a lot to be said for being a speaker. The proliferation of online events has made it easier than ever to be heard by people outside your company and even across the globe. If you've never spoken at an event before it's often best to start out as a panellist. This way you'll be asked specific questions so won't have to prepare a long speech and you'll have other people on the panel with you so you won't be entirely responsible for its success or failure.

The easiest way to get on a panel is to think about events you've attended and enjoyed, contact the organizer and let them know you'd be interested in being a speaker any time they're looking. Give them a few subjects you'd like to speak on, the key points you'd cover within these and, crucially, why you think this would appeal to their audience. If you have a strong social media following or think you'd be able to help them sell tickets in some way, tell them that too. The biggest problem most event organizers face is: how do we tell people about the event and get them to come? If you can help them solve that, you're halfway there.

For larger industry events you might want to prepare a speaker pack. This is a one- or two-page PDF listing out who you are, what you specialize in and what you can speak about. If you've got a couple of 'off the peg' talks, even better. And best of all, footage of you speaking. Most online events are recorded so if you do one, it's always worth asking the organizer if you can have the footage to add to your 'showreel'. This means that when you're pitching for speaking slots in the future you have something to show them to prove you know what you're talking about. N.B. You are never too young or too junior to be a speaker! Make that part of your personal brand and use it to your advantage; you could be the voice of challenge in a stuck marketplace or the Generation Z who explains modern marketing to a backward sector. I promise you, right now pretty much any event would take a talk on why TikTok is relevant for a particular industry. Basically, if you're young and can prove you're in touch with a youth trend, events' organizers want to hear from you.

What happens next

So you're out there in the world, you're making your mark in your industry and then one day you just don't want to get out of bed. When you've got an office to get to that might be enough to get you going but when no one will know whether you're working in your PJs or not, it can become very easy for days to pass and for a grey cloud on the horizon to be a permanent rainfall above your head. When you're working from home you have to prioritize your mental health. Let's look at how in the next chapter.

Exercises to help you grow your personal brand

- Write out your personal brand statement in three bullet points: who are you, what do you do and how do you do it?

- What one action can you take this week to give your brand some publicity? Could you engage with a journalist on Twitter? Write a blog post on Medium? Enter an award? Write it down here, set yourself a deadline and then do it.

CHAPTER SIX

MANAGING YOUR MENTAL HEALTH

Working from home is the dream for some but for others the lack of people around them can be devastating. No amount of Friday night Zoom drinks can ever really replace the joy of a good night out and bonding over a shared hangover in the office canteen the next day. Or having regular access to feedback, the ability to share a joke or a bit of gossip with colleagues and see their reaction, or just a good old moan when you're having a hard day. The lack of these can take a massive toll on our confidence. In this chapter, we'll look at the common mental health issues affecting people working from home, and I suggest some structures you need to have in place in order to protect your confidence and your happiness.

We'll be talking about how you can ask your boss for positive feedback and how to believe it when you get it. We'll look at how to set clear boundaries, so you're not working all hours and how to avoid the loneliness cloud when you're spending days by yourself.

Before we get going, a note. In this chapter, I'm going to stay within the common but relatively easily addressed areas of mental health maintenance. If we were comparing it to physical health these are the areas that are similar to a common cold – most of us will suffer from them at some point or other, and if we look after them quickly we stand a good chance of them not getting too much worse. For those of you who know that you have a more serious mental health issue then I urge you to talk to your doctor or therapist about working from home and how to manage it best. The reality for all of us working from home is that we are going to find ourselves more isolated. We will have to reach out to people more proactively and managing our mental health will be a constant line on our to-do lists. If you want to have a successful career while working from home, being able to understand how your own mind works and when it needs a little more TLC is one of the best things you can do for yourself. Those of you who have had to do that for years, regardless of where you work, will probably already know much of what is written here. Whatever your situation there are useful tools to take away in this chapter but if you are finding it hard to break a cycle of low mood, always talk to your GP or a healthcare professional.

The truth of working from home means that there will be days where you can feel it taking a toll on your mental health. When you first work from home you'll almost certainly make the silly mistakes we all do – you'll get so wrapped up in your work you'll forget to take breaks. It will rain for a few days in a row and you'll suddenly realize that it's been a week and you've had no fresh air. The lack of anyone saying, 'I'm going to get a coffee, does anyone want anything?' will mean that you actually drink less caffeine but also less water. All of these are little things that make a big difference to our mental health, but the good news is that once you've had a few days of feeling tired or unable to concentrate, you'll realize what's going on and you'll find a structure that helps you remember the benefits of fresh air and water.

Unfortunately, there are also other, less obvious structures that working in an office gives us and without those we can often feel burned out and lacking in confidence. I know, you thought that getting away from your colleagues would make life easier but it turns out they were actually providing a vital service and you hadn't even noticed.

One of the things we never praise our colleagues for is giving us an understood benchmark. When you work in an organization you quickly come to learn some simple structures: What time does everyone get into the office? How long does everyone take for lunch? How much time is spent having a joke with the person sitting next to you and how much time is spent with your head down working? What is and isn't acceptable to joke about in the Monday morning meeting? All of these little cues add up to a corporate culture and they make us feel as though we belong. When we start working from home, we might bring some of that culture back with us but we'll also create our own. Only you will know if you spend your lunchbreak watching *Friends* re-runs or going for a long walk, and only you will know if it's acceptable in your 'office' to take a nap afterwards. Only you will be able to decide whether it's okay to play music while you work or log off early if you've achieved a lot in a short space of time. If it helps, I would say all of these are 100 per cent acceptable in my office but often when we're left to our own devices we will build our office culture to be more punishing than forgiving. We'll forget to stop work in the evenings or make it acceptable to just work through lunch without either food or a break. Without people around us to benchmark ourselves against we'll raise the standard we expect from ourselves to an unachievable level and then wonder why we burn out so quickly.

For parents, office life can actually be a break – time away from children requiring all of your attention and a chance to be the person you were before kids came along. When you're working from home it can be much harder to separate the parental you from the business professional. You might find it harder to forget about the argument you had with your child over their homework or the worry you felt about their health when they went off to school with a cold if you're still in the space you associate with them. And of course, if you're having a day when it feels like your parenting skills just aren't up to scratch, it's easy to let that bleed into your working life and make it feel like you're crap at your job too. The reality is almost certainly that you're doing your best but it can be hard to remember that when you're in a silent house by yourself.

If there's anything I want you to take from this chapter it is that working from home gives you the time and space to be kind to yourself. And that your best work will come from this kindness, so start practising it. That doesn't mean that it's okay to put off all your work until your boss is screaming for it or to stop caring about the standards you set – both of those things will cause more stress in the long run so they're not really being kind to yourself – but it does mean that you have to be the one responsible for saying, 'Good job, you've done well today.' Practise that sentence because, as we'll see in this chapter, you're going to need it more than you think.

There are three problems that crop up again and again among people who work from home: perfectionism, a lack of motivation and loneliness. We're going to look at each of these, including how they start out, the impact they have on you and how you can begin to minimize them. See if you recognize a bit of yourself in any of them and learn how to manage that tendency going forward. Let's start with perfectionism.

The curse of perfectionism

Perfectionism runs high amongst people who take their careers seriously; after all, most successful people have had to put in huge amounts of effort to beat off the competition. Being a bit of a perfectionist can actually pay off but when we let it dominate, particularly when you're working from home, it can cause long-term problems which damage not only your work but also your health.

The fact that you're even reading this book tells me that you are somebody who wants to succeed in their career. The problem is that when we have a really strong desire to succeed, it becomes very easy to believe that if we fail at anything, we are letting down that desire. Let me tell you now that that is absolutely not true. There are an awful lot of very average people at the top of business simply because they've caught a lucky break at the right time. In fact, one of my favourite sayings is that when we have as many average women and people of colour at the top of business as we have average white men, then we will know we have true equality.

So, a bit of failure or working at 50 per cent rather than 100 per cent really doesn't hurt. In fact, you can actually learn a lot from it. Learning how to pick yourself up after a failure is the first stepping stone to building resilience. Being able to only give 50 per cent to a project rather than 100 per cent is a step towards knowing how to prioritize your responsibilities. Both of these are key skills if you're going to succeed. So rather than seeing your perfectionism as something that has to be upheld no matter what, perhaps you can start to see now how it might be holding you back.

Of course, it's very easy to say that but very hard to put it into practice. Particularly if, like most perfectionists out there, you're actually in denial about your perfectionism. No good at finishing things? Skip from project to project? Spend days procrastinating? Congratulations, you're probably a perfectionist and you didn't even know it. Perfectionists are not always do, do, do. A lot of their time is spent searching for ways to avoid doing the task in hand. For a perfectionist, the fear that you might start a project and not end it perfectly is so scary, it's easier to just not start. Or to move on to something else before it's finished. Or to decide that you can't possibly start until you've cleaned the fridge. Thoroughly.

Perhaps you can get going on a task but finishing it becomes almost impossible, as there's always something you could tweak. This is the form of perfectionism that we recognize the most, the idea that it's *nearly* there but there's just one more thing... What's actually happening here is that you're allowing yourself to be talked out of finishing. The fear of not being good enough is beating out the fear of taking too long. I once worked with a company where projects were hardly ever actually finished. They would launch a product but then never follow up on how well that launch had gone. They'd write reports but never show them to anyone. There were at least two 'let's review the direction of this project' meetings a week but no actions came from them. The irony was that this company was staffed with truly brilliant people; nearly everyone had a Ph.D and yet none of them could ever get to the end of a project. It was as though they couldn't bear the idea of having to finish something and it not be perfect.

I'm sure that at some point in their lives every single one of them had been able to hand in a finished project but they'd come to work at a place where the company culture said it was better to be perfect than to be finished, and so perfectionism, and an inability to finish anything, thrived. When you're working from home, you need to start to think about how you set your own rules and regulations around what is and isn't accept-able for your own culture. Do you want to be working all hours of the day? Is perfect better than done? Do you want your home to be more home than office or more office than home?

If you really can't let go of the need for perfection then it's time to go and talk to a healthcare professional about that, because you're going to burn out very quickly when you're working from home. If, however, you know this is a problem for you but you feel you can tackle it yourself, then let me introduce you to a concept that can help you: boundaries. And the really good news about boundaries is that being a bit of a perfectionist about them can actually be a good thing.

PERFECT YOUR BOUNDARIES

When we talk about boundaries, what we mean is the ability to set limits that protect your physical, emotional and mental health. This is about being able to say sentences such as:

- 'That is good enough.'
- 'I have to say no.'
- 'I'm going to stop now.'

Knowing how far we can push ourselves, and importantly how far others can push us, is a key component of looking after our mental health. Often, as well as wanting to get everything perfect, we can also want to please everyone. Ironically, push-ing for perfection and trying to keep everyone else happy is an easy way to make ourselves unhappy. So, define your boundaries and stick to them. You'll find that the more you do this, the more people will respect them and the more control you will have over your own time and limits. And if you're not sure where to set those boundaries, then I always like to go back to a question posed by cookery writer Nigella Lawson in a column she wrote. She said, when she's finding it hard to know whether to say yes or no to something, she asks herself, 'What would someone who loves themselves do here?'

If you find it hard to know whether to say yes or no, whether to keep pushing for perfection or to let it go, then ask yourself that question. We're not talking about loving yourself in the arrogant sense of the word but about loving yourself as someone who understands what you can and cannot give, and how to protect your own mental and physical health.

Here are some simple boundaries that you might want to think about when you start working from home.

1. **Establish the times you start and finish work.** It's very simple when we're in an office to know when work starts and finishes because most people are working to the same timetable. Now, we all know that sometimes this results in people working longer and longer hours because if the company culture has long hours, it's very easy to get sucked into thinking that's what is required of you. When you're working from home, however, you get the joy of setting your own hours. After all, there's nobody here watching you. (Actually, sometimes there might be, but we're going to talk about that in the

management chapter and why it shouldn't happen.) It's now on you to be clear and consistent with what works for you. Look back to the beginning of the book, where we talked about working out what your energy levels were at what times of the day. When do you work best? If you could set your hours to whatever you'd like, when would you set them as? Perhaps there are core hours that your company needs you to be online, so think about the boundaries you are going to set yourself outside of these hours. There are lots of apps that will actually monitor your working activity, you can put them on your computer and you can see exactly how many hours, minutes and seconds you've spent on particular tasks. If you're someone who tends to spend too much time on tasks that don't deserve it, think about setting some limits on how you'll spend your time.

2. **When the day is over, tidy away anything that belongs to the world of work.** This was taught to me by my brilliant friend, Anna Codrea-Rado, who runs The Professional Freelancer, a community for self-employed workers that shares wisdom and advice. At the end of every working day, whatever time that is for you, you close down your laptop and you put it away. I know this means you can't browse the internet on your laptop or check your social media, but it also means that you can't have a quick check of your work emails and get embroiled in work stuff when you're meant to

be done for the day. If you find the lure of the laptop too tempting, put either your computer or yourself in a different room. You want it out of sight and out of mind. And if you don't have the space for that, throw a blanket over it, hide it under a pillow, camouflage it within your furniture. Then give yourself 45 minutes of doing something else. It might be reading, watching some TV, cooking dinner, going for a run – 45 minutes away from your computer. If, at the end of those 45 minutes, you're desperate to go back to it, fair enough. But first try putting it in another room.

3. **What you wear counts.** One of the joys of working from home is that on cold, wintery days you can snuggle under your duvet with your cosiest outfit on and not have to leave the house. Equally when it's boiling hot outside you can wander around naked. Just be respectful of your housemates and put some clothes on before that Zoom call. But, if you're someone who finds it hard to get focused, then having a work uniform can be helpful. Putting on the sort of clothes you'd wear if you were going into an office can help switch your mind from home to work. Equally, at the end of the day, changing out of them signals to your brain that working time is over and you can rest now.

4. **Be clear on your working hours – and tell others.** If, as well as working from home, you're also working

non-standard or flexible hours then tell people that and make sure you stick to them. As discussed previously, your colleagues are not mind readers and won't automatically know when you are and aren't working. However, if you start responding to their emails or turning up for meetings when you're not supposed to be there, they're going to assume that you are available at all hours and they'll unintentionally take advantage of that. Get used to saying, 'That is outside my core hours. Here are some times I can do.' Put that 'out of office' setting on your email, and let everyone know when you will and won't be checking your inbox. Add your working hours to your profile on Slack or WhatsApp. Be overly explicit about when you are available and then make sure you stick to it.

5. **Recognize what you need to be okay.** We all know there are things we need to do each day to feel human. We need to get enough fresh air, take some exercise, eat some vegetables and drink enough water. Get the highlighters out and make like you're back at school creating that end-of-year exam revision timetable all over again. Schedule out your day so that every day you get the basic stuff you need to function at your best. And then make this non-negotiable. If you find it hard to find time for yourself – this is a particular problem for those juggling work and caring responsibilities – then it's time to call in the troops. Who can you ask for help? Do you have a

partner who can look after the children while you go to an exercise class or just lock yourself in your bedroom with a good book? Can a grandparent babysit while you go out for dinner? Or if you're looking after elderly parents, is there a friend you can ask to help you with running errands for them once a month so you can gain a bit of time back? Can you use some of your salary to employ a cleaner so the time you spend with them isn't spent doing housework? Remember that you work to live and there are going to be times when it's worth putting a bit of your salary towards some support that allows you to live a happier life.

But what happens when you wake up on one of those days where you know what you need to do but you just can't be bothered? What happens when boredom strikes and never seems to leave? Can you work from home if you've completely lost your motivation?

Finding motivation for the days when you just can't be bothered

If you don't have at least one day where you lie on your sofa watching Netflix and doing the bare minimum to manage your emails, then you can't really say you've ever truly worked from home. However, if this goes on for days and weeks, it might be time to look at what is causing this and just what you're going to do about it.

Low motivation is often a sign that we're simply tired, our body is calling out for some rest and we're not really giving it what it needs. So the first thing to do if you find that you simply can't muster the energy to actually get the work done is to stop procrastinating, and rest. However, rest is not the same thing as lying on your sofa trying to ignore your manager's requests for a catch-up. We have to proactively decide to rest, it can't be something we do by stealth. So the first thing to do is decide for that day you are going to rest and what that means for you. In an ideal world all managers would understand that their team performs better with a bit of rest and so it should be acceptable to email your manager and tell them you're going offline for a bit. But if you have a manager where this doesn't work, you need to manage their expectations. Put an out of office on your email saying you're busy on a project so will only be checking your email at specific times. Move meetings to another day so that you can 'focus without distractions'. Book your rest in for hours when you know you won't be required to sign in or be active online. Make sure that you're not drawn back into working when you should be resting. N.B. I say all this on the assumption that you're a responsible adult who knows not to take the piss. If you're on your twentieth duvet day of the month because you just don't like working, then you might want to find another job.

Now that you've found the time to rest, rest. This doesn't mean you have to go back to bed for four hours, although if that's what you need, go for it. It means giving your brain something soothing to focus on that isn't work. It might be taking yourself off for some exercise. Or doing something creative which doesn't link to work. Or reading a book. Or catching up with a friend. Or doing some meditation. Or sitting in the garden in the sun. Anything that brings your stress levels down and gives you space away from work is rest. By building in time for rest, you'll find it easier to sit down and concentrate when it's time to work again.

USE FEEDBACK TO BOOST YOUR MOTIVATION

If you know you're well rested but you still can't see the point of the piece of work you're supposed to be focused on, then it's time to look at how you're feeling about yourself. Often when we find ourselves procrastinating or feeling a bit low about our work, it's because we're feeling a bit low about our contribution. Think about it: how do you feel when someone praises you and tells you what you're doing is really important? You feel motivated and eager to keep going. But when you're not getting that feedback and you can't see how you fit into the business, it becomes very easy to just give up. However, rather than letting yourself slump, you need to proactively get that feedback that is going to put you back on the horse and set you on your way.

Asking for feedback can be daunting, particularly when you're already feeling a bit low, but if we do it right, it can be the thing that lifts not just our day but our whole career. When asking for feedback, you need to tell the person what you're asking for. So if you've sent off a first piece of work on a new project, received no feedback and are now struggling to keep your motivation up – ask! Email or call the person you need that feedback from and be honest with them; tell them you need to know if it worked for them or not so you can get going on the next stage. And be honest that their silence has made you worry that it's not what they're looking for and that's meant you're concerned about the next stage. Of course, there's the possibility they might come back and say it's not good enough, but at least then you will have a baseline to work from and you can always ask them for guidance.

When we're asking for feedback to boost our motivation, it's worth asking for some positive reinforcement. You might want to ask:

- 'Does this look as good as my previous work and if not, what was it about my previous work that you liked?'
- 'When I'm performing at my best, what do you see in me and my work?'
- 'What situations do you think I perform best in and how could I replicate some of that here?'
- 'What would make this a grade A piece of work?'
- 'What can I do today that would make this exciting?'

Ask people to give specific examples of you at your best. Often your lack of motivation comes down to a lack of belief in yourself and we need people around us to call this out. New parents in particular need this support – looking after a small human who can't tell you exactly what they want but can scream at you when you get it wrong is an easy way to kill your confidence. Just as you needed a kind nurse or friend to tell you that you were doing great with your baby, so you also need a colleague or boss to remind you that you're more than capable at work too.

Feeling like you're not good enough is so often the basis of a lack of motivation. But let me give you a very honest tip here: most of the time, if somebody has hired you to do a job and they are not repeatedly telling you you're doing it wrong, and they are not trying to fire you, you are good at your job.

Let me repeat that: You are good at your job.

But what to do if you have a boss who *doesn't* think you're good enough and tells you that repeatedly? In this case you need to get an outside perspective. Write down the situation you're facing with your boss, including any specific complaints they have against you. Then next to each of these complaints write down whether or not you think they're fair, and why. Be as honest with yourself here as you can. Then take this analysis to someone who knows you and ask them to give you a reality check. Are you being fair to yourself here? Are you being too harsh on yourself or too harsh on your boss? You could be working for someone who is a bully and you need to move on as soon as possible but there could also be some lessons you need to learn. Either way, working for someone who is hyper-critical is very demotivating and you need to tell them that. If they can't hear it and change their approach – and given they're the boss they should have the ability to do this – then you need to seriously think about whether this is the place for you.

BURNOUT

Sometimes, though, stress can escalate to the point where burnout becomes a real possibility. We should be clear here that low motivation is very different from burnout. The official definition of burnout is feeling a lack of enthusiasm and motivation for your working life. I know, I've burned out at least three times today too. In reality, burnout is what happens when we treat our bodies as machines for too long and forget that we're human and need taking care of. Think of burnout as the thing that happens to your car if you never service it or your oven if you never clean it. Too much stuff builds up and we increasingly lose the capacity to deal with it.

This is a particular problem for those high achievers working for companies who don't understand the meaning of 'enough'. If you're a perfectionist you're more likely to burn out because you won't be in an office with other people telling you that it's time to leave or offering to help on projects if they see you are struggling. You are alone with your thoughts and often our thoughts about ourselves are not the kindest.

Burnout cannot be fixed with a few days of holiday. Talk to your GP about taking some proper time off from work and about getting some talking therapy to help you process what led to the burnout in the first place. You'll need to start prioritizing your physical and mental health and there are some suggestions at the end of this chapter for simple ways to do that. Most importantly you need to talk to your company about what is going on. Talk to your manager and if they don't help, talk to HR. Most good employers now know the importance of investing in their team's mental health and they should want to support you. If they don't, then you might want to think about talking to a union or a lawyer about your options. And you definitely want to think about finding another company to work for – you are too important to burn out working for a business that doesn't care.

What to do when the loneliness is too much

Burnout, while dramatic, is fortunately comparatively rare. A far more common mental health issue when working from home – though no less affecting – is how to deal with loneliness and isolation. It's almost impossible not to feel lonely at some point when you're working from home. You're going to miss your colleagues – even the ones you thought you hated. You're going to miss your boss. You're going to miss having that regular feedback and interaction with people. But there are ways of managing the loneliness, you just need to be proactive.

First of all, why do even those of us who love our own company sometimes feel lonely when we're working from home? As I mentioned at the beginning of the book, my belief around loneliness is not that it's caused by a lack of people around us but by a lack of people that we feel we can be emotionally vulnerable with. There is, however, an excellent solution to this and that is: the work wife.

Everyone should have a work wife (N.B. just because it's a wife doesn't mean it has to be a woman; you can absolutely have a work husband too – just make sure whoever you pick is someone you can really be honest with). A work wife is the person you go to when you want to sense-check what you're feeling and get a bit of support for it. They're usually the sort of person you'd have a friendship with outside of the office and you should feel comfortable enough with them to be able to joke around but also admit when things aren't going so well.

Just because you aren't in an office doesn't mean you can't have a work wife. Look for people that you've worked with previously, that you've bonded with particularly well in meetings or that don't work for your company but are on the same career track and understand what you're going through. And then treat them as you would one of your best friends. Check in with them via WhatsApp or social media. Send them the stuff that has amused you in the day, listen to their problems and allow them to listen to yours. Just having someone who feels like they're on your side and will be there to listen to all your work gripes makes a huge difference to loneliness.

And of course, if the loneliness is simply because you're on your own then there are lots of simple fixes. Look for local communities that you can work with. Look for coffee shops where you can meet people. See if you can co-work with people in your area. There are lots of ideas for ways to connect in the networking section. And if all else fails, search YouTube for coffee shop sounds and put that on in the background as you work. Sounds bonkers but I promise, it works!

The final word on looking after your mental health

Years ago, I worked with a mentor who told me that there were five things that protected our mental health, and we should aim for one a day. These are some form of:

- Physical activity
- Human interaction
- Giving back
- Meditation
- Learning

If we did one of those five things every day, he claimed, we'd be giving our brains the best chance of staying healthy. Even better, you really don't have to make big changes to your life in order to achieve this. Here are some ideas:

1. **Physical activity.** You're not required to run a marathon here. It's absolutely fine to go for a five-minute walk around the block or do five minutes of stretching in your kitchen. Anything that gets your body moving counts and after sitting at a desk all day it should feel wonderful.

2. **Human connection.** We all need to feel part of a community – whether that's colleagues, family or something bigger. So book a catch-up with someone whose company you enjoy, have a chat with the barista

in your local coffee shop or just say hi to your neighbour. Remind yourself that you're not alone.

3. **Giving back.** We all get a glow from helping others. It might be donating or sharing a charity campaign, listening to a colleague who's had a bad day or sending your mum a text to remind her that you love her.

4. **Meditation.** I am not a natural meditator at all, and so I really feel for anyone who's like, 'Oh my God, please don't make me sit on a pillow with my legs crossed and my eyes closed, it's really hard.' If you can do that, brilliant. Even if it's only for a minute or two. But if that's not naturally you, find something that allows your brain to switch off and be in the moment. It might be painting, playing music, gardening or yoga (the last two also count towards your physical exercise!). Whatever works for you.

5. **Learning.** This does not mean you have to go and learn a whole new language or apply for a Ph.D – although if you want to, go for it. Really though, learning is just exercising your curiosity. Pick a different section of the newspaper and read it. Ask your social media to share one thing they've learned with you this week. Read a chapter of a non-fiction book on a subject you're interested in. Just stretch your brain a little.

Good mental health when you're working from home can really be summarized as boundaries exercised little and often. Don't make your boundaries so rigid that you can't break them if you need to, or get so concerned with making sure that you're always living a balanced life that you don't allow yourself a little indulgence now and then. And remember to keep asking for feedback – from your boss, your team and the people around you that love you. Often it's easier for others to see if we're treating ourselves with kindness than it is for us to see it. So if in doubt, ask someone kind and then listen to them. Because if you want to have a long and successful career, you're going to have to pay careful attention to your mental health.

You're also going to have to keep an eye on the mental health of those around you. If you run a team you're responsible for making sure that they're all performing to the best of their ability, and that can be hard if you're not in the office with them every day. In the next chapter, we'll look at how you can manage others when you're working from home and ensure that they create the sort of habits and boundaries that allow them to flourish. For now, however, have a look at the exercise below and make sure you complete it – your brain will thank you later.

Exercises to boost
your mental health

What will you do each day, week and month to
protect your mental health? List out at least three
for each category here:

Day: _____ _____ _____

Week: _____ _____ _____

Month: _____ _____ _____

CHAPTER SEVEN

MANAGING A TEAM FROM HOME

Managing a team, particularly if you're new to management, but even if you're not, can be one of the most rewarding or frustrating of tasks. You might see people blossom and grow, you might meet colleagues that change your career or become your boss in the future. And you might also have that one person who makes you wish that the days of drinking whisky in your office at 11am, à la *Mad Men*, weren't behind us. Managing teams can be tough but doing it from home takes even more thought and resilience. After all, if you're at home and your team haven't moved in with you, how are you going to know what they're doing? In this chapter, we're going to look at the basics of good team management. What is the stuff that you need to do, regardless of where you are, in order to manage your team well? We'll look at how we define a successful team, the importance of team culture and how you create it, and some classic management techniques, and we'll apply all of that to a remote-working space.

This chapter will look at things such as how to run one-to-ones, how to build team collaboration and how to manage a difficult colleague. In other words, the sort of things that managers do every day, but perhaps need a little bit of tweaking while working from home. We're also going to look at some of the classic management fears when it comes to remote working. Are you a micromanager? Congratulations, this chapter is where you get to put down your constant need to control people and take a breather. (Micromanagement doesn't work, particularly when you're working from home, so it's time to let it go.)

We'll look at how to get new starters up to speed remotely, how to have great communication within your team, and also how to foster creativity and idea generation when someone's internet is slow. And we'll discuss how to manage those difficult conversations when you're operating in a virtual world. Spoiler alert: sacking someone is just as little fun over Zoom as it is in real life.

Finally, we'll look at how you can support particular groups that might be finding it harder than others. We'll discuss how to create and foster diverse teams. We'll look at how you support younger colleagues who might not have had the chance to learn from their colleagues or see first-hand how a business is run and are feeling a bit lost. And of course, if your business promotes working from home there's a chance some of your team will be doing just that too. How can you support those who are finding it tough and ensure everyone brings their best to the team?

The successful team

First of all, let's look at what makes the basics of a successful team. A good team is one that's working towards a common goal and supports each other in hitting that goal.

So obviously the first thing you need is a goal. As a manager, it's your job to set the one thing that your team is here to do and make sure they understand it. Years and years ago, I had a boss who came up with a slogan, which he would repeat in every single meeting. It went like this:

'Jobs. Sponsors. Membership.'

Three words repeated at every opportunity and we all knew what they meant. Everything we did had to increase either the advertising revenue for the jobs team, the deals revenue for the sponsorship team or the conversion rate for the membership team. And in case we forgot why we were there:

'Jobs. Sponsors. Membership.'

Everyone knew that mantra. He set a really clear goal and made it easy for everybody to move towards it. So when you are thinking about what your goal may be, here are some things to remember:

1. **It needs to be clear.** Ideally it needs to be clear and concise, and easily repeatable. You want your goal to be the thing that people repeat to others, it's an earworm that they just have to pass on.

2. **Everyone should understand how they uniquely contribute to that goal.** So make sure everybody in the team understands why their role is necessary, and the things they have to do to make sure that they hit the goal.

3. **Keep it consistent.** There is nothing more demoralizing than your boss setting a goal one week and then changing their mind the next. So go for something which you know you're going to care about for the foreseeable future.

When a team understands what the team goal is and the role they play in it, magic happens. Everyone feels like they're in a club or a gang of their own, and they know they need to support each other. When we know where we're going and the part we play in getting to that destination, we have a purpose. And purpose is the bedrock of motivation. So if you want a motivated team, set a clear goal.

You'll also need to create clear goals for individuals. (We'll look at how to set key performance indicators later on in this chapter.) Agree them with your employees, and then have an open discussion about what happens if they're not met. Why were they not met? Were there particular circumstances? Did you perhaps underestimate the amount of time something was going to take? Was it impossible to get it done in that time, or was it, quite frankly, down to the fact that the employee wasn't working hard enough? All of those are possible explanations, but they need to be discussed between the two of you.

So now you've got a goal, the team needs to talk to each other about how they're going to achieve that goal. We'll talk more about communication structures and how to implement them later on in the chapter, but a successful team is one that knows how to communicate with each other. A good team almost has an inbuilt language and tone: they know when they're joking, they know when they're worried, they know when something is important, and they know how to get that across. That's because they spent time thinking about how to create communication structures that work for all of them.

The final hallmark of a successful team is the ability to disagree and still support each other. If you have a lot of very smart, opinionated people in a room together, at some point they are going to disagree. Conflict is not bad but it needs to be managed.

When your team disagrees with each other it's your job to bring them back together. First of all, go back to the goal. Do they understand what the goal is and how to prioritize their actions to ensure it's met? Secondly, remind each of them how they uniquely contribute to the goal. Just because one of them is going to come out of this disagreement feeling like the winner, doesn't mean the other person's role is invalidated – in fact they're more important than ever because the winner of this difference of opinion is almost certainly going to need the support of their team to make their idea happen. And then remind both of them of the other's strengths. You have no control over whether members of your team like each other but you can try to instil a sense of respect amongst them. Just remember, conflict happens but it needs to be managed.

Creating a team culture

All successful teams have a strong team culture. We tend to think that in order to create a team culture, we need people to be in the same room as each other. But team culture is not created by buildings, it's not something that leeches from the walls and we absorb by being in a particular meeting room at just the right time. Relying on an office to create a team culture is just lazy – a foosball table doesn't have the power to make or break your team.

If you want to create a strong team culture wherever you are, you can't expect it to just happen. You've got to work at it and keep working at it. You actually have to design it. If you want somewhere to start, go back to the chapter where we talked about our own values. Now think about using those exercises to identify your team values. If you were to pick three or four values that you want your team to have consistently, what would they be? Set them out, make sure everybody knows them, and then stick to them.

You might have seen in some people's houses those annoying signs which say, 'In this house, we do fun, love, laughter, joy', etc. Well, this is the moment for your team to have one of those signs – metaphorically speaking; please don't actually buy them one. 'In this team, we do…'

Be clear about the values you choose for your team and the definition of those values because, as we know, some people view values very differently. Work with your team to identify the values that define you and then make sure people stick to them. If people transgress those values, pull them up on it. Remind them of what the team values are and how important they are to the culture of the team.

One of the most important ways to build team culture is through trust. A horrifying trend that emerged when lots more people started working from home was managers using spyware on their team's computers to see what they were up to. I am a hard 'no' to this and if you or your company have resorted to it, I am now giving you a hard stare. If you're worried your team is so unproductive that you actually have to spy on them, then you might first want to look at your own management techniques.

By putting spyware on an employee's computer you are a) showing them you have no trust in them and b) showing yourself that you don't believe you are capable of managing them remotely. You do not need to use spyware to get your team to work hard. On the contrary, the second you put spyware on your employee's computers, you are telling them that you view them as unreliable or lazy – and people often live up (or down) to our expectations.

Finally, think about how you can build your office culture when remote working is the default, and office working is the exception. I think this is going to become more and more necessary as remote working increases, because if the majority of your team are remote, that's the working pattern that should drive the culture. For example, all meetings would be done on video call. If you happen to be in the office, and you want to go to a meeting room and do your video call from there, fine.

It might be the default that all social events are done remotely as well, or perhaps that you have team catch-ups on email or Slack rather than in person. Whatever it is, assume that remote working is the norm, and office working is the exception. If you do that, you'll create a team culture which works for everyone, regardless of where they are.

The management basics

When you step up into a management role, you will, if you're lucky, be taught some basic management techniques. But this isn't a given and when we're dealing with other people it's useful to have some basic strategies in our back pocket to help manage them effectively. I'm going to look at two of them here, particularly in relation to remote working. Remember that when you're working from home nearly every form of management will need a little adjustment, and a lot more communication.

THE IMPORTANCE OF KPIs

KPI stands for key performance indicators, or if you want to look at it this way, the things that need to happen in order for an employee to show that they are doing a good job. I think it's absolutely vital when working from home that everybody knows what their key performance indicators are. You might want to set these by year, but break them down so they are, at the very least, quarterly, if not monthly. Making sure that everyone clearly knows what they should be achieving means that if they don't reach their goals, it's clear to both parties that there is a need for a conversation. It stops things drifting. When we have key performance indicators, people don't get distracted by side projects. They don't lose sight of the end goal. They are particularly important when you, or your team, are working from home because they give you a clear idea of what everyone is up to without you having to stand over them.

When you're thinking about setting KPIs, make sure they are specific and measurable. All those KPIs where the wording is something like 'to be better than we are now' can go out of the window. Better is subjective but clear numbers, dates and achievements are measurable, so get picky about how you set your KPIs. 'Improve by 10 per cent' is a specific goal; 'increase by 50 per cent' is a specific, if stretching, goal. 'Set up 10 per cent more meetings with prospective customers' is an even more specific goal. If you can measure them, then you can see where you started and where you ended up, and nobody can argue with the numbers (well, they will but KPIs make it that much harder).

Give your KPI a deadline. Some people like to work on a clearly outlined, step-by-step plan. But others of us, and I include myself in this, tend to prevaricate right up until the last minute. We will do things seconds before the deadline and be racing to finish them. And if there's no deadline then the project will rumble on forever. Setting people deadlines makes it clear when something has to happen but your role as the boss is then to step back and allow them to do it in any way they wish. Lots of research shows that there is very little difference between people who plan things out and people who do it at the last minute in terms of results. But there *is* a big difference in terms of performance if that deadline isn't there. As infuriating as it might be to see someone drifting along as if they had all the time in the world and then racing for the deadline, or to watch someone diligently plan it all out leaving no room for experimentation or thinking, if you step in and try to micromanage, both sides will be frustrated. It will appear that you have no trust in your team and, as we discussed earlier, trust is a prerequisite for productivity. So set a clear deadline, have regular check-ins if that makes you feel more comfortable, then allow them to get on with it.

One final point on KPIs: if you have an outstanding team performer who meets their KPIs in half the time that anyone else does, this is not a reason to give them more work. Just because they work faster than anyone else doesn't mean that you should then decide to give them twice as much work, unless they really want it. This ability to hit a target ahead of deadline generally means they're very efficient. They get shit done in a time the rest of us can't. Good for them. Give them half a day off. Let them take some more holiday. Or give them the jobs you need done quickly. Whatever you do, don't punish efficiency; we need more of it in the workplace. Don't pile the work on for being fast. You'll just end up with people saying, 'Sod it, I'll take longer.'

RUNNING BETTER ONE-TO-ONES

The golden rule of home working is more communication, as much as possible. So setting up one-to-ones with your team is a priority and you need to make them sacred. Most of us will have had a one-to-one with a boss previously. You will know whether or not you have a good boss by how you view a one-to-one. Is it an interesting and informative discussion where you both learn from each other and you feel like you leave with clear feedback and clear goals? Or is it a slightly awkward catch-up where nothing is really said, and you leave feeling like you're not quite sure what to do next? If it's the latter, the one-to-one is not working. Don't be that manager. Let's stop the cycle of terrible one-to-ones here.

As a manager, your job when creating a really good one-to-one is to set the tone and expectation for that meeting. While some people like to wing a meeting, I think it's important to send an agenda for your one-to-one in advance. If you don't feel you have time to do this, ask the member of staff to draw one up 24 hours in advance. You can then check whether there is anything you want to add or go with the agenda as set. Either way, both of you know what the format will be.

The second rule of a good one-to-one is that you should listen more than you talk. Oh my gosh, I can't tell you the number of managers who feel like they can talk their way out of the one-to-one. Stop talking, start listening! Ask questions, be curious. Don't assume you know why your team member has done something or what they want. Leave space for them to talk and when you think you've left enough space, leave some more. The brilliant thing about this is if you can learn to leave silence between remarks, you'll probably find out way more than if you fill the gaps. Most people find silence very difficult and they'll leap in with information to fill it.

Thirdly, encourage honest conversation. In order for honest conversation to happen you have to build trust and a sense of psychological safety. That means the person has to feel that you're not going to use what they say against them or pass it on to others without their consent. You're the manager now; you need to let the days of office gossip go. Equally, if somebody tells you something that you don't like, you can't snap at them for it. Try to find out why that's their view – maybe you've missed something and they're giving you important information? Whatever happens, try not to break the circle of trust unless you know you're happy to lose that team member.

Finally, save five minutes at the end to write down the agreed steps that will come next. What have you talked about? What will be done? Who will do it? When will it be done by? When will you check in again? One-to-ones should be ideally once a week or at least every other week. If somebody is struggling with something, give them more check-ins. If it looks like someone is really underperforming you need to not just bring it up in a one-to-one but also follow it up with an email. Encourage your employee to do the same, and make sure you correct anything you disagree on and keep a note of it. Keeping good meeting notes ensures there's no confusion about what was and wasn't agreed further down the road. We can all miss things in meetings or forget what we've agreed to, so a written record ensures everyone is on the same page. And if the situation escalates and you have to look at an official performance warning, or even letting them go, then you have all the evidence ready to go.

So how do these one-to-ones change when you're doing them remotely? The one thing that shouldn't change is that they're face to face, even if it's over a video call. Try to avoid doing them on a phone call where you can't see the other person's face.

I feel really strongly that we need to cut time off every meeting that we have. You might notice when you work from home you start doing more one-to-one meetings with people than you would when you're in the office. That's because you don't have those little water cooler moments where you get to catch up. Because you're having more meetings, those meetings need to be shorter. For official one-to-ones make more time, although maybe 50 minutes rather than an hour (see page 48). For unofficial one-to-ones, those more casual check-ins, 25 minutes is fine. You're just sorting out a quick issue or making sure someone is okay, this doesn't need to take an hour.

A simple way of cutting your meeting times is to set your calendar to automatically assume that all meetings are 30 minutes long. Yes, you can do that. Aim to keep all meetings 25 minutes or 50 minutes. Time between those meetings allows you to regroup, step away from your computer, rest your eyes and come back refreshed for the next one. In the virtual world, meetings might be more frequent, but they should be less time consuming.

How to face the fears of managing a remote team

There are a lot of people out there who think managing a team remotely is not a good idea. I can totally understand why the thought of being a manager when you or your team are remote can be really terrifying. After all, if the buck really does stop with you then it feels an awful lot safer to be in the same place as that buck and see exactly what all the other people handling it are up to.

There are some classic fears that come up for managers either working from home or managing staff working from home. The first one is that we believe that if we can't see people, we won't know what they're doing. It's logical. But also, do you really know what your team is up to when you see them in the office? If you were to put spyware on your office-bound colleagues (which, as we've discussed, you absolutely shouldn't!) you'd probably find that far more of their time was spent Googling holidays than you'd expect.

The second one is a fear of miscommunication. We worry that we won't get our message across because we're not in the same room as people – what happens if they don't get our tone or misread something we've put in a casual chat channel? When we're working from home we need to work on our communication and take extra measures to make sure both that we're heard and that other people feel heard. People can feel left out if they sense we're not communicating with them enough. So we need to work harder to ensure that we are clear about what we mean and that people feel connected to us.

Finally, we worry that creation and innovation will disappear if we're not all in the same room, brainstorming away with Post-its, together. The reality is that you might not feel the chemistry or excitement instantly but it's still possible and in this section we're going to look at how.

MOTIVATING YOUR REMOTE TEAM

Has anyone seen that fantastic Michelle Pfeiffer movie where she is a teacher in a failing school, and she's assigned the worst class in the establishment? They're all failing students, and she walks into the class, and says that everyone from that moment has an A. Their job is not to work for an A, their job is to work to keep the A. Well, make like Michelle with your team. Assume that they are all A-grade staff, and their job now is to keep that A. Some of them will drop below and if they keep dropping then you'll need to consider whether you want them on the team (not all of Michelle's students made it to graduation, sadly) but for now assume they're an A.

However, if someone is going to keep their A then they need to know when things are going wrong. Embed honest feedback into your team culture, make it a value. In her work, the speaker and author Brené Brown extolls the concept of 'generosity'. She sees generosity as giving honest feedback in the spirit of wanting to make someone better and them accepting the feedback in the spirit of wanting to be better. We all get this wrong sometimes; not all feedback is delivered well or from a place of clear understanding. But if we try to give feedback from a place of generosity then we have a greater chance of giving our team good feedback and helping them keep that A.

This means we have to be clear and specific in our feedback. It's not enough to say to somebody, 'This piece of work isn't good enough.' You have to tell them why it's not good enough and what you wanted instead. If what you wanted was not clearly communicated at the beginning, then you also have to take a level of responsibility for that. You have to say, 'I was not clear when we spoke.' By owning your part in this you encourage your team to own theirs too.

Some people find it easy to encourage their team and terrifying to critique them. If you fall into this category then the good news is that your team almost certainly enjoy working for you. The bad news is that they probably don't do as good a job as they could do. Learning how to give constructive, critical feedback is crucial for any manager. If you find it hard remember this: in the long run your team will go further in their careers if they're given the opportunity to correct their mistakes and learn. It's your job as their leader to help them grow, not keep them stuck in mediocrity. Learn to reframe critical feedback in your own mind as a way to help your team progress – you'll probably find this helps you accept criticism better too.

Finally, create a sense of psychological safety with your team. Allow them to fail and say that failure is okay, but we have to learn and grow from it. If you do this, you'll find that they're more open with you and come to you earlier with the things you need to know. If you're not going to be in the office, you need to encourage people to come to you but if they're going to do that they need to feel safe. That means not blowing up at them if they've done something stupid, listening before shouting and helping them work towards a solution. This doesn't mean that you don't get to feel and show your frustration but make it clear they aren't being thrown out of the group for screwing up. They're still a part of your team and they still matter. Because when teams don't feel safe, they hide things, they keep secrets. That's when we run into the problem we're going to talk about next.

NO MATTER WHAT, KEEP TALKING

What does good communication look like when working from home? A former boss once told me that the first rule of good communication is understanding that brevity, while useful, is not the same as clarity. I think this is brilliant and have tried to use it subsequently. Brevity can be useful, and often desirable, but clarity is the goal. How clear you are? This is something that it's good to get some feedback on either from your team or your boss. How clear is your communication style? Clear communication is the right information given at the right time, in the right way. Nail that and you'll have knocked one of the biggest issues of work, from home or anywhere else, on the head.

Let's look at the right information – that is to say, what are the key things that people need to know? First of all, think about who you're communicating with, what they are concerned with, what they need to know and what might they have picked up from other people that you should repeat here? If you're not quite sure, ask yourself if you're writing to a superior or someone on your team. If it's a superior, ask yourself: if somebody was to quiz them on this, what would they look silly for not knowing? If it's someone on your team, ask yourself: what do they need to feel safe here and how much am I willing to share with them, bearing in mind that they might tell the rest of the team?

Now you've got the right information, it's time to deliver it in the right way. Different methods of communication work better for certain things. I'm going to be honest: I don't think difficult or bad news is communicated well over email. You can use email to warn of bad news – 'Things are not going well on this project, we need to have a discussion about it. Can we set up a video call?' – but the bad news itself needs to be in person.

You can, however, communicate success in an email, that's very different. Being able to say, 'We've finished this project early and the client is delighted,' or 'We wanted you to know that our sales targets have increased by 10 per cent this year.' Whatever it is, people like good news and they like it instantly. Don't book a time to deliver good news, just pass it on as soon as you can – so get typing. The recipient should be excited about receiving it, they'll forward the email, they'll tell other people. Plus, just as it's useful to keep a written record when things aren't going so well, it's useful to have that same record of your team's successes. It's easy to forget the stuff we're good at so writing it down – and keeping it somewhere you can easily find it again – is a good way to create a bank of brilliance that you can look back on when times are tough.

Do also be generous with that brilliance. If your team has smashed their targets and you're emailing the boss to tell them, make sure you copy them in. It will let them know you're proud of them and are championing them, plus it will give them a chance to receive any praise from higher up directly.

This formula works across all mediums – anything that needs time and thought or that might cause panic or fear if you're not there to set the context, do it in person. Anything which will please people can generally be done in written format. This does assume a level of common sense, though: post a particularly explicit meme on the company Slack channel and you're on your own.

Finally, timing is everything. Unless it's an emergency, don't give any big information at 4pm on a Friday, when people are off for the weekend. And definitely don't send one of those, 'Let's have a chat when you're in on Monday' emails. What does that mean? Why are you telling me this on a Friday afternoon? So I can worry about it all weekend?! I like to think good news should be conveyed on a Friday: send everyone into the weekend feeling proud of themselves and get the bad news over with early on in the week but not so early that you don't have time to warn people about it.

It's only polite to give people warnings if you are going to have a difficult conversation with them. Tell them what that difficult conversation is about and anything you're going to need to know from them. Don't spring things on people because it works for you. Unless it's part of a wider appraisal strategy, it's simply not fair and no one will show up at their best.

Finally, don't schedule important meetings before lunch or complicated ones after. We're only human, we can't be our best on an empty stomach and we all need time to digest.

Encouraging creativity from home

For many years I worked with advertising firms, trying to convince them that a more flexible form of work would pay off in productivity. The same argument came back every time: you need to have people in the same room if you want to generate creative ideas. Is it possible to be truly creative or innovative when your team is remote? Honestly, I think yes. And the brilliance of some of the ads created during the global lockdown proves this to be true. Sometimes we're more creative with some restrictions imposed upon us. I know it doesn't feel quite the same. There is something exciting about being in a meeting room with a group of people, where somebody has a great idea, and you get to build on it. That excitement can take a bit more effort to create over a video call. But you can do it.

First of all, the same rules apply for all creative thinking from home as they do anywhere. It's okay to fail. Bad ideas are welcome. Encourage experimentation. Allow people to throw stupid ideas out there and tell them they're great. Build on people's ideas. There is a lovely coaching philosophy which can be summed up as 'What I like about that is…and…' After every idea, ask people to come back with what they like about it and then build upon it.

What I like about this is that it gives the person whose idea it was a sense of confidence but it also forces our brains to look for the interesting part of an idea, to look for the thing that could work rather than deleting it altogether.

It can be harder to build that creative chemistry on a video call but you can encourage it outside the meeting. What are your Slack channels for fun and entertainment? How do teams get to know each other? Make sure new employees have a buddy to help them understand the culture. Maybe think about reiterating your values at the start of a big meeting, so that people remember what they are aiming to encapsulate. Encourage people to break out into smaller groups so that they all have time to contribute.

Also, if you are doing some hardcore creative work, make people take screen breaks regularly. Get them to move around. Don't expect people to sit in front of their laptop to do it. Encourage the same level of informality and movement that you would if you were meeting in person.

Finally, celebrate the good ideas. Do something together – book a tea and cake hour and send everyone in your team a box of cakes to enjoy. Take an early end to the day and actually be together – whether that's going for a drink, an event or just for a team coffee; tell people about it on the various communication channels you have, shout about it and be proud of it. Celebrate creativity exactly as you would if you were at the office.

How to manage a difficult team member

Dealing with difficult colleagues is one of the most challenging things for any manager, regardless of whether you're in the office or working from home. You are always going to have one member of your team who for some reason does not feel like the easiest person to manage.

When you are managing someone difficult, check how they are as a person versus how you are as a person. Is there stuff in them that you find particularly triggering that is simply part of their personality? Perhaps they are somebody who is a bit more negative or serious. Or do they joke around when you prefer people who just put their heads down and get on with the work? Be honest with yourself about whether they're really difficult or whether you just don't like them. It's okay not to like people you work with but you do have to try to respect them.

However, if they are really underperforming, you need to have a conversation with them about that. It's helpful to approach this in a structured, methodical way; this will reduce the stress on both you and the employee because everyone will know where they stand and what the next steps are. Take your time to prepare before the conversation and, if it helps, run through what you want to say with the human resources team or a more senior colleague first.

First of all, check your expectations against theirs. If you set them a task and weren't happy with the result, ask them what they think had to be achieved? Were you clear about what you saw as the expected goal? Also, look at whether you're measuring output or hours – is it simply that they are not available online in the afternoons, but actually, their work is really good? Look back over your calendar history and see how much time you have spent communicating with them. How many one-to-ones do you have with them? How many informal conversations? Be honest about whether or not you have tried to build that relationship.

One of the big things we can see from people working from home is a sense of isolation. Perhaps they don't feel they're being included or made part of the group. If you haven't been giving them enough feedback, they might be suffering from imposter syndrome or feeling that they're not a valued member of the team. If they are constantly worried they're not very good at their job, they might unconsciously decide to peel back from it. Give them encouragement and support and see if they improve.

If they don't, it's time for them to move on. Make sure that you speak to HR first and get clear on the process. It will save you a lot of hassle in the long run: HR will have dealt with this before and will know how to support you. They should also know all the legal ramifications and be able to advise you on what to do to avoid the risk of any counterclaims from the employee.

When you have the conversation with the team member, be clear and concise. This is not a time for that classic management technique of the shit sandwich. 'You're really good at this, but actually, we hate you and we're firing you. But don't worry, you're still a great person.' Not here. It's brutal news and you're not going to make it better with platitudes, you're just going to confuse them and drag the process out.

Give them the facts, tell them what's happening and the reasons for it. As with any meeting, make sure that when you leave, both of you are on the same page. They're definitely going to feel miserable but know that you might too; it's never nice to fire someone even if you're desperate to be rid of them.

But if somebody is not right for the team, they'll be feeling it too. In the long run, they'll be able to move onto something better suited to them.

Wherever possible, try to have these meetings in person; video calls have a terrible habit of freezing at the wrong moment and can make a difficult meeting feel even more impersonal. If you can't meet in person, however, there are some simple things you can do to make the call easier. First of all, make sure you've tested your wifi and your connection earlier in the day; if things are playing up try to reschedule. Do the meeting somewhere quiet where you won't be overheard and nobody is going to wander past and see your screen. Keep a note of any key points you want to make by the side of your computer and refer to it regularly. Make sure you leave space for the other person to speak and keep a note of what they say. As ever, follow up with an email but check the wording with HR first. If it's the company practice to record video calls then do so here but only if it's something you do regularly – you might think you want a record of the call but it's only going to make it more awkward for both of you if you feel like everything you say is going to be saved for later analysis.

How to build an inclusive team from home

As a manager, part of your job is ensuring that all of your team is working to the best of their ability. But, when we are working remotely, there might be some people that we sort of miss out on. To build happy and productive teams, we also need to build inclusive teams. There is a lot of talk at the moment about diversity and inclusion in the workplace – gender, race, socioeconomic background, age, neurodiversity, the list keeps growing – and you need to make sure that your team achieves this. Partly because working in a team with different backgrounds and skills is more interesting, partly because we know diverse teams produce better results but mainly because it's the right thing to do. For too long workplaces have been filled with people who looked alike, came from similar backgrounds and had similar views on the world. But if a company really wants to be fit for the future then it needs to understand the power of bringing in people with different life experiences and offering the same chances for advancement to everyone.

To do this you need to be aware of your biases. We know that in the UK, people with a non-Anglo-Saxon name have to apply for 60 per cent more jobs before they get a positive response than those with an Anglo-Saxon name. In the US, racially marginalized job seekers who 'whiten' their names are more than twice as likely to get an interview. When you see a name pop up on your screen, what do you think? Do you instantly assign them a gender, or a race, or an age? It's not bad if you do, we all do it but we can't let those decisions influence what we then think about that person. In fact, I would challenge you, if you know you have certain expectations about people, see how often you can prove those expectations wrong. Be aware, look at your colleagues. Does everybody look the same, sound the same, have the same background? Be honest with yourself if you're not doing enough to create a diverse team. The Harvard Implicit Association Test is a free online test you can take to explore your biases. When you know what they are, they go from unconscious bias to conscious and it's at that point that we can recognize them and ensure we don't act on them. Everyone has biases, they're a way for our brains to quickly process information, so you're never going to be completely bias-free but you can choose to understand them and then consciously act in a fair way.

It's not enough, however, just to have a diverse team. We have to have an inclusive team. What that means for you as a manager is taking a look around and seeing who is always at the centre of things, and who is on the outskirts, and how can you bring them in. This means in meetings, look at who is always talking, and who is silent. Can you call on those people? For those who don't like being called on by surprise, make sure you send an agenda around to all of the team and an email to those people you hear less from that says, 'I would love to hear your thoughts on this tomorrow. Do remind me to ask you or remember to speak up.'

Finally, when people do feel excluded, that might be because they simply don't have the ability to be included in the same way. Think about the different conditions and restrictions people are facing from home. Young colleagues might be in a shared house with lots of other people, so they don't really feel comfortable doing Friday night drinks with you online from their bedroom. Employees with disabilities might need more support with technology and having it adapted to work for them. Parents might need a level of leniency if they've got kids running around the place. Understand that actually, when we allow people to work from home, and when you work from home, you're asking people to let you into a previously private part of their life. When they do that, you have to be supportive of what they need as a whole person, not just an employee.

The youth

Do you remember when you first started out in an office and you didn't know what you were doing? So you watched people and you learned. You went to meetings and you saw how those meetings were run. You saw your boss schmooze their boss and it told you how to build relationships. So much of our workplace behaviour is learned behaviour. Younger colleagues working for organizations where remote working is the norm are not going to see that. So you need to support them in filling that gap.

Obviously, the more feedback you can give them, the better. They might be confused about how to know if they're doing a good job. So set up those regular one-to-ones, make sure you give them detailed feedback and clear guidance on what else they should be doing. Think about all those things you learned that they might need help with. Encourage them to take responsibility for running meetings, talking to clients, or creating reports. But also give them examples of how that's done. Send them emails that you've sent to clients before or show them examples of good presentations. Invite them to do client video calls with you. Invite them to co-host a meeting with you. Give them the chance to set things up and feel like they are learning.

Help them understand the culture. I always think it's really important that there's a buddy system in place for every new employee. Somebody they can ask questions of, the sort that are not on the new-starter forms. Like, is it okay in meetings to speak up? Or, is it okay to send an all-group email? Or, what do we do on Fridays if somebody has done something really well? All of those kind of cultural questions that they might not understand. Give them a buddy who can give them this insight into the organization, and who they're not going to feel threatened by.

When your team just want to be in the office

Not everyone wants to work from home but if your company has decided to go remote you might have team members who need more support in making the switch. Remember that working from home often leads to isolation. Go back to the chapter on mental health and think about all those things that I suggested you do in order to look after your own mental wellbeing. All of your team need to be doing those things, too. Check in with them about whether they are taking regular exercise or if they have somebody to talk to. If they don't you might want to ensure they're bonding with their assigned buddy and possibly help them broaden their network.

Take them back to the values of the team. Remind them how they fit into it and what their role is in meeting the goal. They're not just out there on their own doing their work, they're actually contributing to something, and their team needs them. Think about how you can build them up in team meetings or celebrate something they've done, so that that feeling about being out there alone, not really contributing to anything is diminished.

Finally, keep giving regular feedback. Remember, when people are on their own, they create stories in their heads. Those stories are so often self-deprecating and not true. But when we've got nobody to tell us otherwise, we believe them. Regular feedback, giving them the space and time to ask questions, to check some of those stories they might be making up, to air their feelings of imposter syndrome, will help immensely. Sometimes when we speak about a problem we instantly feel relieved and better. And if we have a manager who can show us we're worrying about nothing, even better. They're your team, support them.

Exercises to make you a more effective manager

- Feedback is important, as I've mentioned a few times! But as a manager it's important to get feedback on yourself too. Who can you get this from? Write down three people who can give you some useful feedback on your management style and a date by which you will have spoken to them.

- After reading this chapter, what have you noticed about your own management style? What could you be better at? Note these down here and next to them make one commitment on how you will improve going forward.

CHAPTER EIGHT

MOVING ON

So you've sorted out working from home now, you've built a brilliant remote-working team, and you made it all the way through your career plan. But now it's time to move onto the next thing. In this chapter, we'll look at how you assess a future company's working policies, how to ace a remote interview, negotiate a salary that reflects the impact you'll have and not how much time you'll spend in the office, and how to talk about working from home upfront so that you and your future employer don't have mixed expectations.

Moving on when you have a flexible working arrangement can feel scary. Men tend to move jobs more often than women and one of the reasons for this is that women are more likely to have negotiated working from home or part-time hours and they're loath to jeopardize that. But as more and more offices embrace remote working, open international offices which require navigating different time zones, and actually realize that people are happier and more productive when they have a choice over the way they work, so it becomes easier to talk about this and ask for it in a job interview. And frankly, if your future employer is so concerned about where you are and when, do you really want to work for them?

The job-hunting basics

You've had a good run in your current role but it's become clear that you need a new challenge/can't stand your boss, so it's time to move on. Rather than just pulling up LinkedIn and heading for the jobs section, it's worth doing a bit of prep first to define what it is you truly want. Quite often when we're ready to move on, we see a job we like the look of and just apply for it. We don't give enough thought to what our priorities are and, out of these, which are non-negotiable. Before you even get started on the job hunt, you need to know these two things, so let's take some time to work them out.

THE PRIORITIES

When you're applying for a job you need to know what it is that really matters to you. In both your actual life and your working life, what are your priorities? This is about going back to your values – you might want to look at the list you completed earlier on page 68. If you haven't already done so, note down the values that really matter in your work and in your personal life: if you're going to have a happy life as well as a good career you want a company that reflects both of them as much as possible. Then think about what you currently like about your working situation and how you're going to make sure that your next job replicates it. Perhaps you currently work from home three days a week, and that's perfect for you and exactly what you want. Or if you work flexible hours and you need that, or really like the level of competition or the spirit of collaboration – whatever you like about your current job, add it to a list. This is your priorities list. Then you want to put that list in order of importance. What are the benefits or features you must have in your next role and what is up for trading if the job is worth it? It's time to get brutal about what you really care about.

It's okay for some of your priorities to not turn up in your next job. It might be that your next employer will say, 'Actually, we can only give you two days working from home,' but the salary is so huge, you can't turn it down. Or you just really love the company and you're desperate to work for them, so you'll negotiate on something else. The point is to work out what is the stuff that's important upfront so that you don't lose all of it. If you lose sense of your priorities, you're going to find that you don't really enjoy the job, no matter how good it is. Instead, you need to look for something that aligns with most of your priorities, if not all of them.

THE NON-NEGOTIABLES

Now you've got your priorities, it's time to work out what the non-negotiables are. What are the things on your list you absolutely cannot shift on? This can be work and life. So if it's really important to you that you work for somebody who is inspiring and visionary, and you turn up to the interview and the person who's going to be your boss seems a bit dull, it's not the job for you. Equally, if it's really important for you that you are home at 3pm every day to pick your kid up from school, then you need to make sure you talk about that in the interview and see what the reaction is. There's no point finding your dream job and then realizing that everybody works 14-hour days and you'll never be allowed to leave the office.

I'm not saying that there is *never* any room for non-negotiables to move, but really, the clue's in the name: it has to be a case of absolute last resort. What you want is a job that's going to give you both the work and the life that you love, so start thinking about what that looks like now. Far too often we drift into a job because it's the obvious next step on the ladder or because everyone else thinks we'd be mad to pass it up. But taking a role without really analysing whether or not it fits with your career, and life, priorities might actually set you back on achieving your bigger dreams.

Reading the job

So you've worked out what your priorities and your non-negotiables are, now it's time to go out and find a job. But how can you tell if this is going to be a role that will both fulfil you and work in the way you want to?

When you're actually looking for a job, it's really important to listen both to what they're saying and what they choose not to say. What I mean by that is a lot of jobs will tell you,

'It's the greatest lifestyle; you'll have the best fun; it's the most collaborative of teams' – all the good stuff. They'll sell you the dream upfront. But you also need to think about what they're not saying. What do they fail to mention? Do they not talk about flexible hours? Do they not talk about remote working?

Listen to what they emphasize the most. If they emphasize how brilliant a team they are and how successful they are, that means they're really driven and they're really goal-orientated, which could be great – but if it comes at the cost of collaboration or working styles, and those are non-negotiables, then it's probably not the job for you. Does anyone talk about their families or life outside of the office in the interview? If so, you'll know you're in a company where it's probably okay to take time off to go to your child's school play.

If you go into the office, take a good look around. How noisy is it? Do people seem to be chatting to each other or is it more of a heads-down environment? Take a look at what people are wearing. Get a feel for the vibe of the place. Even if you don't go into the office, you can still get an idea of the sort of place it might be. I was once doing a video call with a company where everybody was wearing suits, even though they were all working from home. So every day they were getting up, putting on a suit and not going anywhere in it. That clearly worked for them. They all really liked it. But as a long-term place for me, I knew it wasn't going to be right – most days, I'm in jeans. Depending on how the video call is set up you might be able to see something of the meeting room. Is it colourful or more muted? Can you see yourself sitting there? There are lots of clues about a company's values to be found both in person and on a video call, you just have to trust your instincts.

And of course, remember the golden rule of all job hunting. If you decide you're going to go for a job, negotiate for what you want upfront. We'll talk about how to do that later in this chapter but don't take a 'We can assess that when you're in the job' on something that is a non-negotiable. People are much less likely to accommodate your requests when you're in the job than when you are being interviewed for it. At that point, you're still the shiny new toy they really want and they're much more likely to give in to your demands or at least consider them. But once you're in there, then you're just part of the corporate furniture. It's going to be much, much harder to renegotiate your role from that point onwards. So be upfront about what you want, and if they really can't do it, you have to think about whether it's a non-negotiable or something you're willing to sacrifice.

Investigating a would-be employer

There's a very weird piece of corporate culture which makes it almost unacceptable to talk about things like salary, working policies, remote working or flexible hours in the first job interview. I think this is a bit ridiculous, but honestly, some people will react really badly to it. So you're better off just learning about them and the company in your first interview, and then if you go to a second one, bringing up the rest of it.

However, if you don't want to waste your time on a second interview with a company that won't entertain any of your non-negotiables then there are ways you can get a sniff of how they will react.

First of all, look on their website. A lot of companies will have a job section, which will tell you about what it's like to work there. Have a read of that. As before, look at what they talk about and what they miss out. What do they emphasize? What are the words they use? Look for any overlap with your values. See if you can get a feel for what the company culture might be like.

Then, if you can, see if you can find a friend of a friend who works there or has worked there, and get the inside story. This is what all that social media stalking of your ex has trained you for – if you can track down their new girlfriend on Instagram, you can definitely find an approachable employee of your dream company on LinkedIn. Obviously, everyone's experience is different, but getting an actual person who works at the company to tell you what it's like is going to be much, much better than just asking in an interview. In particular they should be able to give a good assessment as to how the company will or won't meet your non-negotiables. I think this is particularly important for working parents; if you can find another parent who can give you an honest view on the work/life ratio or what happens when you come back from parental leave, then this is gold. Too many companies have fantastic parental policies on their websites and zero idea of how to enact these in practice.

How to ace a remote interview

Remember when we talked about the window-dressed, video call nook? Now is the time for the nook to come into force. Get it fully prepped, make sure you're comfortable and that you're showing off the best of you – both your face and your background! When you're in an interview you don't want to be worrying about 'Is my computer perched in the right place or not?' Test it all out and make sure you feel completely comfortable and secure in your choice of location. And if you're not sure whether or not to put that crazy coffee-table book with the amazing cover out in full view, maybe don't on this one. A bit of personality is great, but you've only just met these people, so keep your deep and abiding love of Japanese cats in costume for later on in the relationship.

There are some obvious things you need to do but they bear repeating: make sure you're inside with good wifi. Check your wifi at least an hour before. See if you can arrange a video call with a friend an hour before to make sure your internet connection and computer are behaving as normal. Check, check, check. Make sure, at least on your side, it's as clear as possible. Do the call inside and close the windows, yes, even if it's boiling hot. What you don't want is the sound of a siren zooming past, just as they ask a critical question.

If you know you're going to be doing lots of job interviews or if you just like looking good at meetings, think about investing in a webcam that you can position to get your best angle. Most of us are just using the video on our laptop or computer, which, quite frankly, doesn't show us at our best. Mostly you'll be looking down into it, which is never a great angle. With a webcam, you can get a much more flattering angle. It makes you look much more approachable and, sadly but truthfully, you're more likely to get a job if the interviewers think you look presentable. The world is a ridiculous place sometimes.

Just remember, anything new needs to be tested at least five times before you can rely on it for a job interview. Think about when you do it in person. You wouldn't wear a new outfit without road testing it first. So, test, test, test. Disconnect your phone, close down your email and any messaging platforms. In fact, I close down everything that isn't related to the interview; you don't want to be distracted by the constant ping of your email. If you have your phone connected to your computer, think about disconnecting it for the time of the call. You don't want people ringing you in the middle of a job interview.

If you have to give a presentation, have that open and ready to go, and make sure you're aware how the particular platform you'll be using for this interview works, so you can upload it smoothly. So if they've told you it's going to be a Microsoft Teams meeting or a Cisco Webex meeting, have a little play around with those platforms before, so you can practise load-ing and uploading your presentation until it's second nature.

Look at the webcam on your computer and not at the people on the screen or, worse still, yourself. If you can, put a sticky note over your own face – it's just too distracting. Stick a gold star just below your webcam to remind you that this is where to look, just test it first to make sure you're not accidentally covering the camera. When we're looking into our webcam, it appears as though we are looking into the eyes of the people on the other side. We appear engaged and interested. Nobody's asking you to stare into it for the entirety of the interview; you can look away, but keep coming back to it. It'll give great eye contact and make you look interested in the conversation.

The advantage of interviewing from home is that you can have some little cheats to help you along. If you know there are some particular things you want to hit on your CV, write them down in bullet point format and put them to the side of your computer or in front of you. What you don't want is to be constantly looking down and reading so set up some big, clear reminders – 'Made X thousand on this job' or 'Worked for these three companies' – so you'll be reminded to hit those key points. It's much better to go for prompts rather than a fully written article, because if you write it out in full, you'll sound scripted and they'll notice.

Asking to work from home

So you've found a job you love, the feeling is mutual and you're on the way to your next role...but how do you bring up working from home? In truth you can bring it up at any point, although as I mentioned before there is a cultural hesitation about this so don't worry if you feel uncomfortable doing so in the first interview; you're not alone. The key is to find a way of scoping out their views on the subject before showing your hand.

In the first interview you can get a feel for their attitude towards working from home by asking more general questions about working practices. Ask them, 'What is the culture here like? How should I expect people to behave in my first 90 days? How do you onboard new starters? What do you do if somebody is struggling with the work? What do you do if somebody is achieving in their work?' Ask questions that allow you to understand their company values.

When you're onto the second interview, and you know you're interested in the role, then you can be more direct. Try saying:

- 'My previous company promoted working from home, so I'm used to doing that. What's your policy on this?'
- 'Previously I've worked remotely, how would you feel about me doing that in this role?'
- 'What is the working culture here like and how do you prefer to work?'

You're unlikely to get a clear, 'Yes, we love remote working!' from these questions, unless the job spec has specified that's what's wanted here, but you'll be able to tell from their answers how open they are to it. Do they have a 'preference for people being in the office' or perhaps they're 'open to remote working but we're a bit slow on the uptake of it' – in both of these cases you're going to have to work a bit harder to convince them that remote working is the way forward.

If, however, they've given you an answer that suggests they're pretty open to a conversation about it then it's time to get your ducks in a row. Remind yourself of your priorities and your non-negotiables. How many of your priorities does this role tick? Is it enough for you to be happy doing the job? Now look at your non-negotiables: are they still set in stone? Is there anything you might be prepared to move on slightly and what is an absolute deal breaker? In negotiation terms, we're looking at what you're able to give to make the deal happen. It might be that they agree to all your terms straight up but if they don't it's good to know what you're happy to let go of ahead of things, so you can offer them up some alternative situations that you know you're okay with.

Be clear in your requests. What do you want? Write it out beforehand in a notebook and bring your notes to the second interview. Ask for more than you want (both in terms of working style and money) and be prepared to negotiate. It's unlikely you'll get everything but if you've worked out what you can give way on, you should be able to find a good compromise.

When you're talking about remote working with a future employer who might be sceptical of its benefits it's good to remember the point we made back in Chapter Two: don't focus on why it's good for you, focus on why it's good for the company.

Have some examples ready of how you've made working from home a success in the past. Explain how you managed teams, got projects through to completion or increased profits – all while working from your home office/bed (don't mention the bed). Show them how you're more productive and what that means in terms of outputs. Explain how it improved the productivity of your team and changed working practices, and then explain how you'll do this for them. Be clear that you don't see working from home as a lifestyle choice but an essential part of modern working that improves businesses and adds to the bottom line. Think of yourself as a cheerleader for working from home, relentlessly optimistic and convinced of the brilliance of your team. And if your would-be employer really can't get onboard with this then you need to think honestly about whether this is the job for you. Could you suck up working full time from an office for a few years for the advantages it brings? Or are there going to be better opportunities elsewhere? Whatever you do, don't go in thinking things will change once you're in the job – as Maya Angelou said, 'When somebody shows you who they are, believe them the first time.'

Often at the negotiation point, employers will try to use working from home or flexible hours as an excuse to bring the salary down – don't accept this! There is an idea that if you're working four out of five days, then you should accept a 20 per cent drop in salary. Have they taken 20 per cent off the job description? Are you expected to do 20 per cent less work? Are your targets 20 per cent lower than anyone else's? If so, then I'd consider it, but if the drop in salary is entirely down to the time you're working remotely, you should definitely push back on it.

Flexible hours are very rarely as flexible as they claim. There's a strong likelihood that you're going to find yourself working outside your agreed hours, that there will be meetings or away days that you'll be expected to attend even if they're on your days off. Taking a pay cut and then feeling as though your company is constantly taking advantage of you will build up resentment towards your employer very, very quickly.

Instead of just accepting the pay cut, try this instead: a brilliant and very senior woman took on a CEO job four days a week. They offered her 20 per cent less pay than was being advertised. Her response was: 'We both know that there are going to be occasions where I need to do more than four days a week. I don't want us to ever be in a situation where either I resent you for taking that time or you resent me for refusing to work it. So, I'll take 10 per cent less on the understanding that we both want this relationship to get off on the right foot.'

I dare you to ask for the full salary on this basis.

Your first days

So you've made it through the interview, you've thoroughly vetted them and now you're on your first few days. How do you get settled in and make sure all your colleagues under-stand your working practices? Obviously, this is much easier if you've chosen to go to a company where remote working is the norm. If this is the case, your biggest priorities are getting used to the company culture and adapting to the tech they use – I have yet to find two companies that use all the same tech in the same way. If you can find a buddy to help you negotiate your way through this, then great. But also use your newbie status to start building those relationships. Set up lots of one-to-ones and informal coffee video calls, ask people for their top tips for working at this company. A great question is: 'What's the one thing I should know that nobody will think to tell me?'

If, however, you're one of a few people working in a 'non-standard' manner, you're going to have a little bit of prep to do with your colleagues to get them used to how you work. The first thing to remember here is that if you treat it as though it's perfectly normal, so will pretty much everyone. You might get a few comments along the lines of, 'Working from home? Does that mean you're actually working on those days or not?' But do your best to be patient with them; one day these people will be converted to working from home too and then they'll be eating their words. In the meantime, assure them that working from home does indeed mean working and yes, you'd still like to be invited to meetings on those days, you'll just dial in instead of being there in person.

The second thing is to start as you mean to go on. You might find that your new employer suggests that you do the first week in the office, and if you can make that work and you think it would be beneficial, then go for it. It can be helpful to get an idea of the culture and to meet a few people but try not to let it go on beyond that. You want to get people used to your working patterns and the quickest and easiest way to do that is to apply them. Go back to looking at your boundaries and make sure you've clearly set them so everyone can see. Put your working hours in your calendar and your email signature. If someone invites you to a meeting on a day you don't work, push back on them and either change the day or change the meeting to a video call. Whatever you do, don't sneak your working from home. Don't change your days to make meetings or pretend that you'll see everyone tomorrow if you're not going to be in.

For decades women have been sneaking out of the office early just so they could go and pick their kids up from school, while the men have been swanning out high on their sense of self-worth for doing a basic bit of parenting. Well, in this case the men are right. We all need to be proud of the commitments that we work around and stop trying to hide them in the background, hoping no one will notice. You are setting the standard for every home worker that comes behind you so be the pioneer that you wish you'd had earlier in your career. Help younger colleagues working from home to negotiate the office politics around it. Offer it up as an option to all of your team and encourage them to try it out if they're curious. Be an advocate for your own way of life because if you can't do that, who will?

What to do if it's not working out

At some point in our working lives we all make a career choice that on reflection wasn't the best one. This is particularly easily done if you're someone who works from home, is keen to find another job and jumps at the first one that offers home working without a fight. For most people what happens is either they discover that the company and the culture isn't for them or they realize that while the company might talk a good game when it comes to working from home, the reality is very different.

If you're experiencing the first problem, then remember you are not alone. Nearly all of us have jumped into jobs because it seemed too good an offer to turn down, only to find there was a reason they were offering so much. The first thing to do is have a good look at what isn't working for you here. Do you feel it doesn't match your values? Are your priorities or non-negotiables being challenged?

Once you know what isn't working, do talk to your manager about it. Even if the problem is them! That's what they're there for and they should be able to help you find a solution. The clearer you can be on what the problem is, the easier it's going to be to resolve it. 'I'm just not sure the job is what I thought it would be' is a lot harder to solve than, 'I'm not feeling a lot of collaboration in the team, I don't know how to bring people onto my projects.' Try to name the problem and an example. It might be that your manager already knows this exists as a problem within the company and together you can work to solve it. Or it might be that they don't see the same problem you do, in which case you have some thinking to do.

If you've found yourself at a company that claims to be pro working from home but gives all the good projects to people who are in the office 24/7 and leaves you out of key meetings and updates, then you've found yourself in a classic case of 'death by good intentions'. The background to this problem is almost certainly that someone higher up in the company recently decided that the working culture needed a shake-up and that every manager should review how their team works. A new set of guidelines was probably produced in a very pretty brochure to go with this and suddenly the company was making all the right noises about flexible working, which was what you heard when you joined. Unfortunately, people are slow to change, so while the policies might have updated, the people hadn't. The good news is that if their hearts are in it you might be able to bring them onboard.

You'll have to lead on this, setting really clear boundaries and constantly reminding your colleagues of them. You might want to encourage a few people to try out working from home or set up a Slack or WhatsApp group for those of you who do to encourage each other. This is basically a long game: people will come round to your strange ways eventually, it's just how much patience you have.

There is a chance of course that new policies have come in and people are paying lip service to them but have no intention of changing their ways. You'll probably be able to feel if this is the case but a good clue is if you talk to your manager about it and they have no interest in resolving the problem. If they tell you to lump it or leave it, you know which one to pick.

Whatever situation you find yourself in, know that it's always okay to say, 'This isn't for me,' and move on. There is a lot of talk about it looking bad on your CV to have a quick move. I would suggest that one quick move can be easily dismissed and that your happiness is more important than a perfect CV. If you find yourself moving several times in quick succession, however, you might want to ask yourself, 'Is it them or is it me?'

The most important thing to remember is that one bad experience does not mean that working from home is forever gone from your life. More and more companies are moving to a remote style of working and there are more opportunities out there than ever before. Just make sure to do your research, take the time to find the right place for you and set your boundaries from the outset. So, take heart, your dream job is on the horizon.

Exercise to identify your priorities and non-negotiables

What are your priorities and your non-negotiables? List them out here and then be sure to check back in with them. Even after you've landed your dream job!

CHAPTER NINE

THE FUTURE OF WORK AND YOU

In this book we've worked through the cycle of working from home, from knowing if it's for you, talking to your boss about it, working out what you really want from a career, managing a team and finally moving on. You should now be all set for a future filled with the working practices you want in your life and the ability to work from wherever, whenever. But, of course, nothing stays the same and as more and more of us work from home so we will start to find that working patterns and trends change. Some will be for the better but if we don't keep a close eye on them, some will also be for the worse. In this chapter we'll look at what those changes might be and how we can start to protect against some of the bad ones and usher in the good.

The good

There is always a moment in the development of a trend when it passes over from the obscure to part of our normality. Working from home isn't a new development, we've been doing it in higher-paid jobs since the 1990s but even before then women were taking in laundry, sewing or even doing admin and secretarial work that could be conducted at home to make ends meet. We've always known there was an advantage to being able to conduct our business from our homes but the trend towards fancy offices and a desire for managers to feel in control led us to abandon this. And of course, so much of what our society deems as normal is defined by what men do. Men go out to work and therefore 'going out to work' is seen as the way it should be. During the global lockdown of 2020 I found it interesting to see the male leaders that were almost shocked by how much better their lives were when they didn't have to commute and could actually spend quality time with their family. Of course, not every man felt this way, one friend told me about her boss who was back in the office the day lockdown was lifted – apparently his home life wasn't quite so chipper.

Working from home has often been seen as a woman's choice, something she does to juggle the combined roles of motherhood and work. In reality, women chose to work from home for all sorts of reasons beyond childcare but now that more men are taking up the banner of working from home too, I think we will finally start to see a shift in how employers understand home working and ambition. After all, the stereotype that men are burdened with is that they must be ambitious, so just as CEOs would once have thought women choosing to work from home was a sign of a lack of ambition, perhaps now they will realize that ambition is not dampened by your location.

One of the trends that working from home is leading to is the expansion of what and where 'home' looks like. 'Working from home' now means working from your local coffee shop, a co-working space or even the beach, and I don't think this is going to stop anytime soon. The rise in co-working spaces has allowed businesses to save money on expensive office space and employees to build connections outside of their own company. As more of us choose to work remotely so there is going to be an increase in the ways available to do that. Private members' clubs catering to specific industries or professions are on the rise, and there are even travel agencies dedicated to remote workers who want to travel while they work – not only will they book your hotel and sightseeing trips, but they'll also organize co-working spaces and meeting rooms in whichever city you want to visit next.

Traditionally our choice of home has been limited by the need to be somewhere close to work. But if we can now work from home, and if technology can place us virtually in the same space as anyone else, then our horizons are flung wide open. When the pandemic hit and everyone had to work from home, house prices in the most beautiful, and remote, parts of the country went up. Rather than having to stay in the big cities to find work, young people were going back to the towns they grew up in and staying there. Instead of being surrounded by built-up areas, most of us wanted to be somewhere where we could experience nature, feel the fresh air on our faces and generally live in a rural idyll. Of course, this is much more appealing in the summer when the 20-minute walk to the nearest neighbour feels like a golden adventure, than in the winter when it's pouring with rain or you have to dig through a foot of snow to get outside your front door.

One of the advantages of this migration back to our hometown is the rise of a local economy. During the 2020 pandemic local businesses reaped the rewards of having people at home. Rather than buying our groceries from big supermarkets we started to go back to the greengrocer at the bottom of the road, we bought our coffee from the local bakery rather than the big-name chains and supported those businesses physically closest to us. After decades of industry and entrepreneurship being congregated in major cities, we are starting to see the rise of industry hubs in small towns again – and that has to be good for all of us.

Long term we will see a shift in where people live and how important to them it is to be near the office. And if companies want to retain the best talent then they are going to have to buy into this shift too. Too often business has had the upper hand in the negotiation – 'If you want to work for us then you need to be in the office' – but as more and more people move further away they'll have to make a choice between the best person for the job and the closest person for the job. It will be interesting to see who they choose.

If we're all scattered all over the country, we'll probably find ourselves working with people that we've never met and who possibly have completely different lives to us. I think it's exciting that home working could actually be the one thing that opens up diversity in business. When I was working as a diversity consultant one of the problems businesses often moaned about to me was that they didn't get enough range in the socioeconomic backgrounds of the candidates that applied for internships. Given that many of these interns then went on to get jobs in the company, it wasn't surprising then that many of them looked the same as their boss and had often gone to the same school. It didn't seem to occur to the people running these internships that they lost out on legions of brilliant applicants who couldn't afford to give up a secure job in their home town and move to a big city where they would have to pay expensive rent and accommodation, to take up a low-paid internship that may or may not lead to a 'proper' job. As the trend for remote working increases so we might, hopefully, see a trend in bringing on interns that don't need to uproot their whole life just for a bit of work experience.

This experience of working with people we've never met before, often from different backgrounds is, I believe, going to do wonders for our communication skills. We'll have to learn how to work with people that we don't know intimately. If you can't have those chats over the coffee station, if you don't know how they like their tea, the getting-to-know-each-other process becomes longer and more thoughtful. We won't be able to make snap decisions about others, instead forming an opinion over time. I genuinely believe that more space between us will actually bring us closer together and create longer-term and deeper working relationships. A girl can dream, can't she?

The bad

Of course, with the sunshine has to come a little rain and we've already had some warning droplets. The most worrying trend is the change in job allocation. Because if you can do your job from anywhere then why would a company pay your rates to keep the job in this country, rather than farming it out to a country where wages are much lower? We've seen this happen to call centre jobs and while the belief has always been that jobs in the 'knowledge economy' are safe, I think as we become more globalized this is going to be the case less and less often.

There are two ways to look at this that allow for a little positivity. The first is to realize that if jobs can move country, so can you. Why are we all holed up in small flats in a country with a rainy season that lasts at least six months when we could be on an island paradise somewhere? Barbados offers remote workers a one-year working visa, allowing you to live on the island as long as you're working for a company or running a business that's based off the island. Why aren't we all in Barbados right now?

If, however, you're not as tempted by the thought of a rum and pineapple at a little bar overlooking the sea as I am, then the good news is that even as the world has internationalized and jobs have moved abroad, so other jobs have sprung up. Nature abhors a vacuum and this is the same for the economy. Keep your skills up to date, be open minded about what you do and know that something else will come along – it always does.

An element of positivity is necessary for all of us in the working world because things change very quickly. As we've already discussed, building your network is essential because your boss may move, your job may change, or you may decide to quit – nothing is ever fixed. Knowing this and being okay with it is a key part of managing our mental health. Be prepared for whatever's round the corner: have a savings pot, keep growing your network so you have people to call on and don't get complacent. Flexibility is the future.

A final word to businesses

This book is aimed at those currently working from home or those who want to work from home, but it wouldn't exist without companies who allow their staff to do that. The number of companies embracing remote working has grown far faster in the past year than at any point in history but this speed often means that some of them don't know how to do it well, so let me quickly use this space to give you some pointers.

1. Someone wanting to work from home does not signal they don't have ambition or they want to put their career

on hold for a bit. It MIGHT mean that but unless
you check with them you'll never know, so park your
expectations at the door, open your ears and listen.
You'll be surprised how effective that is.

2. You can't usefully manage home workers with the same
    targets you've been using on your office workers for
    decades. Trying to replace 'How long are you in the office
    for?' with 'When were you last online?' is a metric that
    is only going to make everyone sad. Use the suggestions
    in Chapter Seven to help you move from measuring
    presenteeism to productivity, and see how that changes
    everyone's behaviour and boosts your bottom line.

3. Don't throw the office out completely. Companies that
    overnight decide to go remote find it hard to make it
    work. Offer flexibility, try to organize in-person events
    (and offer a travel budget for these) and remember that
    we all need to get out of our own four walls occasionally.
    Just don't put any store by who is and isn't in your office
    – most of the time they're just there for some company
    and are doing more chatting than working anyway.

Returning to the office

However much you love working from home you might find
that there's a point when you go back to spending the majority of your time working from an office. Maybe your home

situation changes, or your dream job requires you to do it and you're happy to compromise, or maybe you just fancy a change of scene for a bit. Whatever the reason, if you've been working from home for a while there are a few things you might have forgotten and need to keep at the forefront of your mind.

1. Expect to be tired, at least for the first few weeks. Being back in an office is going to give your brain a lot of stimulation. There is the commuting, the people, the noise – constant stimulation, which if you've been living a peaceful life at home with just a dog for company is going to feel like a lot. Your body will respond to this and you're going to need to ramp up the sleep and the self-care. No wild nights out for a few weeks, at least until you feel settled in.

2. Think of the lessons you learned from working from home and bring these into the workplace. Shorter meetings, more one-to-ones and setting clear boundaries around when you are and aren't available. If these things worked for you from home, then they will work in the office – and you might even find yourself changing the working culture because of it.

3. Appreciate that you can work in both ways. Can you put in a case for home working, just for a few days a week? Your ability to flex between home and office is a gift, so don't waste it.

Make WFH work for you

I believe that working from home offers choice, freedom and the ability to find the perfect work-life blend that works for you. That is the most important part here – *works for you*. Don't expect to get it right first time, shift things around a bit until you find a system that supports your energy and your productivity, and allows you to find some freedom in your work.

As a human I have a tendency to be a bit all or nothing. When I first started working from home I veered from working from 6am till 10pm, to having weeks where I lay on the sofa and tried to recover from my work binge. Who I was showed up in the way I chose to work. Inevitably I didn't manage this for long. I had to learn to regulate my working hours, set myself small tasks to feel like I'd accomplished something and realize that I couldn't reward myself for every email answered with a handful of M&M's. Working from home held a mirror up to my habits – good and bad – and forced me to figure out which ones were valuable and which ones weren't. It will do the same for you.

So, treat yourself with kindness. Know that you might put on a few pounds when you first start working from home but that you'll also lose them when you finally replace the chocolate chip cookies with a walk around the block. Accept that you might spend your first few weeks 'working' while watching Netflix – sometimes a series is just too good to stop. Expect to row with your partner or housemates about exactly where you can put your work stuff and when you do your video calls. And know that all of this will work itself out in the wash.

Now go sort out your Zoom nook, order a supportive chair for your back and get back to work: you've got this.

ACKNOWLEDGEMENTS

The first thing to acknowledge is that this book wouldn't exist without the creative brilliance of the team at Quercus but in particular my publisher Kerry Enzor. Thank you so much for trusting me with your idea and letting me write this. Huge thanks also to Lindsay Davies for your brilliant editing and manuscript polishing; the book is one hundred times better because of you. To Tamsin English for combing through it and spotting all the many times I repeated myself, and Elizabeth Ana for making sure people know it exists. In fact, a big thank you to everyone at Quercus; you've made writing a book fun, fast and exciting, exactly the opposite of how I thought it had to be. I'm so lucky to have been able to work with you.

In the book I talk about the need for cheerleaders and I'm lucky enough to have the best squad out there. To Char, Elle and Vix; thank you for being the best friends a woman could have, for the endless messages of support and love, and for realising early on in lockdown that you could send alcohol via Amazon. If home is where the heart is then you will always be home to me.

I never thought I had the patience or commitment to write the number of words it takes to make up a book so I need to thank my oldest friend, Emma, who knew from the age of seven that it would happen. Sometimes someone else having faith in you is stronger than having faith in yourself; thank you for doing that for me.

For Judi, Lottie, Jules, Zoe, Iso, Ellie Pike, Daniella, Nikki, Hannah, Angelika, Debbi, Emma S, Emma S and Nat – thank you for all your wisdom, support and general amazingness over the years. Most of the ideas in this book came in some way or another from all of you. I'm just sorry that I couldn't remember which ones and credit you appropriately; feel free to take that up with me over dinner.

As I was growing up, my parents ran their business from our home for several years. They were quite clear that this was a terrible idea and I should go and get a corporate job in a big shiny office where someone else was paying the electricity bill. Sorry for ignoring your advice on this, and most other things, but look, I got a book out of it!

Just before I started writing this book, I acquired an at-home support team as well as a remote one. To Tom and Blue, you are the best home colleagues. Thank you for putting up with me being a grumpy mare while writing this book, for constantly providing me with food (Tom), reasons to leave the house (Blue) and cuddles when I was tired (both of you. But mainly Blue). You, literally, saved my life in the middle of all this. I'm so lucky to have you.

And finally, thank you to my home. The best thing I ever did was investing every penny I had, and quite a few I didn't, in you. To anyone reading this from the discomfort of a crowded houseshare, or their parents' spare room, or fearing how they are going to make next month's rent and what that means for keeping a roof over their head: I see you. Hold onto the dream of a room of your own, it's coming.